SUCCESSION PLANNING

AN ANNOTATED BIBLIOGRAPHY
AND SUMMARY OF
COMMONLY REPORTED
ORGANIZATIONAL PRACTICES

SUCCESSION PLANNING

AN ANNOTATED BIBLIOGRAPHY AND SUMMARY OF COMMONLY REPORTED ORGANIZATIONAL PRACTICES

Lorrina J. Eastman

Center for Creative Leadership
Greensboro, North Carolina

The Center for Creative Leadership is an international, nonprofit educational institution founded in 1970 to foster leadership and effective management for the good of society overall. As a part of this mission, it publishes books and reports that aim to contribute to a general process of inquiry and understanding in which ideas related to leadership are raised, exchanged, and evaluated. The ideas presented in its publications are those of the author or authors.

The Center thanks you for supporting its work through the purchase of this volume. If you have comments, suggestions, or questions about any Center publication, please contact Bill Drath, Publication Director, at the address given below.

Center for Creative Leadership
Post Office Box 26300
Greensboro, North Carolina 27438-6300

CENTER FOR CREATIVE LEADERSHIP

CCL No. 324

Library of Congress Cataloging-in-Publication Data

Eastman, Lorrina J.
    Succession planning : an annotated bibliography and summary of commonly reported organizational practices / Lorrina J. Eastman.
       p. cm.
    ISBN 1-882197-06-2
    1. Executive succession—Planning—Bibliography. 2. Executive succession—Planning. I. Center for Creative Leadership. II. Title.
Z7164.07E23 1995
[HD38.2]
016.6584'071248—dc20
                                                        95-16258
                                                              CIP

Table of Contents

Preface

This report was originally written for participants in the Center's course, "Tools for Developing Successful Executives." In this program, human resources executives and career-development professionals learn to apply executive-development practices (such as learning from experience) and instruments (such as 360-degree feedback) to develop organizational leaders. Maxine Dalton, Program Manager, assigned me the task of acquiring and annotating literature that has practical implications for succession planning.

While I was preparing the bibliography, I noticed that certain practices appeared repeatedly. My advisors and I concluded that descriptions of some of the most common of these would be helpful. Thus, the report has two parts: Section 1 is the annotated bibliography and Section 2 contains descriptions of the commonly reported succession-planning practices found in the fifty-six works.

Reaction to this report has been so positive among "Tools" participants that the Center has decided to offer it to a wider audience.

I am grateful to several individuals from the Center who made this report possible. First, I am indebted to Maxine Dalton, who provided me the opportunity and encouragement to write this report. For their feedback and insightful comments on earlier drafts of this report, I would like to thank Richard Campbell, Frank Freeman, George Hollenbeck, and Russell Moxley. For their assistance and patience in helping me identify and obtain references on succession planning, I would like to thank Peggy Cartner, Kelly Hannum, and Carol Keck. I am also grateful for the invaluable editorial guidance which I received from Bill Drath, Marcia Horowitz, and Martin Wilcox. Finally, a special thanks goes to Cindy McCauley for her constant support.

Introduction

Succession planning is crucial to the long-term viability of a company. Its purpose is to assure the continuity of an organization's leadership by identifying and developing potential candidates for key management positions (Buckner & Slavenski, 1994). Rothwell (1994) defines succession planning as "any effort designed to ensure the continued effective performance of an organization, division, department, or work group by making provision for the development and replacement of key people over time" (p. 5).

There is a growing interest in this topic and a need for more information on how to establish, implement, and evaluate appropriate systems. This report provides a summary of selected works on succession planning for positions in middle to upper-level management. It aims to provide human resources managers and other executives concerned with succession with an entree into, and a general understanding of the nature and extent of, the practical literature on succession planning.

The report is in two sections: Section 1 consists of an annotated bibliography, which summarizes fifty-six works; and Section 2 describes eleven themes, which organize the commonly reported practices.

References were derived from a literature search of both academic- and practitioner-oriented sources. Psych-Lit (January 1987 to June 1994) and ABI-Inform (January 1987 to June 1994) databases were searched for recent references. In addition, sources were drawn from a comprehensive bibliography of over 400 references on executive selection and succession planning, which was released by the National Academy of Public Administration (June 1992).

It is important to emphasize that this annotated bibliography is not intended to provide a comprehensive or critical coverage of the succession-planning literature; rather, it is a collection of references that should be useful to practitioners seeking more information on the subject.

The general criterion for choosing an article or book for annotation was that it include practical suggestions or implications for succession planning for a broad range of management positions or that it focus on the developmental component of succession planning. More specifically, I selected a reference for annotation if it met at least one of the following criteria: (a) The work discussed the linkage between management development and succession planning; (b) the work addressed why succession-planning systems often fail; or (c) the work described the practices of organizations that have experienced success with their succession plans.

It is also important to emphasize that the eleven practices in Section 2 are not presented as a blueprint for success; rather, they are meant to inform the reader about what practices are commonly reported in the literature.

Section 1: Annotated Bibliography

This section annotates fifty-six articles and books that were derived from a literature review on succession planning. Reports, journal articles, book chapters, and entire books are summarized. The annotations are in alphabetical order by the first author's last name. To find a listing of all the authors and a complete list of titles herein, readers are referred to the Indexes at the end of this book.

William R. Allison. The next generation of leaders. *Human Resource Professional,* Fall 1993, pp. 30-32.

Allison describes how succession planning typically focuses on replacing positions as they exist at present. This method is based on the premise that the organization is trying to clone today's successful executive and that it lacks forward thinking about organizational changes and demands. However, with radical changes going on in businesses, both the requirements of key positions and the skills and abilities required of people in them will change drastically, and succession plans must reflect these changes. Most plans emphasize the needs of the organization, but the individual needs of managers should be considered as well. Finally, the author suggests that in order to develop a broad set of competencies, high-potentials should be provided with the opportunity to work in three or more functions with assignments that last a few years in each function.

✣ ✣ ✣

Timothy T. Baldwin and Margaret Y. Padgett. Management development: A review and commentary. In *International review of industrial and organizational psychology* (Vol. 8). C. L. Cooper and I. T. Robertson, Eds. Chichester, England: John Wiley & Sons, 1993, pp. 35-85.

This three-part chapter provides a comprehensive review of the management-development literature from the past five years. Part 1 reviews general skill taxonomies for managers and the assessment of effective management, with an emphasis on the changing managerial environment and the concomitant need for new models of effective management and new assessment strategies. The traditional core competencies of managers are not wrong or invalid but only incomplete. In particular, "learning how to learn" is expected to become an increasingly important macrocompetency for managers. Multiperspective feedback from subordinates, bosses, and peers (that is, 360-degree feedback) is also growing in popularity as a powerful assessment tool.

Part 2 reviews the context of managerial learning, with a strong emphasis on job assignments, on-the-job experiences, and relationships as opportunities for management development. In part 3 the authors discuss emerging issues in management development: Firms are demanding development that is results-oriented and aimed at implementing business strategy, and managers are expected to take responsibility for their own learning.

Richard W. Beatty, Craig E. Schneier, and Glenn M. McEvoy. Executive development and management succession. In *Research in personnel and human resources management* (Vol. 5). K. M. Rowland & G. R. Ferris, Eds. Greenwich, CT: JAI Press, 1987, pp. 289-322.

The focus of this chapter is how organizations can "capture information about managers and plan for their orderly movement to top-level executive jobs." The authors provide a diagnostic model of executive development/ management succession, which includes six components: (1) executive role, (2) role requirements, (3) organizational opportunity, (4) executive/ organizational match, (5) transition mechanics, and (6) consequences.

Briefly, the model can be summarized as follows: Effective executive development requires identifying executive tasks and roles and then specifying the requisite skills and temperaments for successful performance (the authors review the literature on executive role requirements and requisite traits and competencies). However, it is not enough to understand the nature of competencies and traits required for successful performance. An additional issue is the organizational context: the organization's culture, life-cycle stage, technology, degree of risk associated with decision making, and the type of feedback cycle should all be considered. The assessment of executive/ organization match should involve comparing each potential executive's skills-and-competencies profile with the organization's requirements in terms of tasks, roles, culture, risk, feedback, and technology.

Transition mechanics are related to three topics: succession planning, skills assessment, and skills acquisition. Succession planning is a subset of the overall human-resources planning process, which is illustrated by the authors' succession-planning diagram (p. 305).

Effective succession planning requires the formal assessment of candidates; individuals are then nominated for succession, entered into the executive-development system, and eventually placed in upper-level positions. Skills assessment focuses on the performance and future potential of employees and is based on information, such as performance appraisal, assessment centers, and psychological tests. Skills acquisition (executive development) can be enhanced through rotational assignments, formal training, performance feedback from various sources, and mentoring (though authors caution that, currently, purported advantages of mentoring are more anecdotal than empirical). Consequences of executive development/ management succession include compensation, social relationships, and physical and mental health.

Charles Borwick. The logic of succession planning and why it has not worked. *The HRPlanning Newsletter.* Part 1: October 1991, 12:9, pp. 1-5; Part 2: November 1991, 12:10, pp. 1-5; Part 3: January 1992, 12:11, pp. 1-5.

Borwick discusses, in a three-part series, what he has learned from his experiences with over one hundred succession-planning systems.

Part 1: The traditional approach to succession planning was established in the 1950s and is based on a reductionist philosophy that matches people with statically defined positions. However, this approach conflicts with the rapidly changing needs of today's organizations; it is also inconsistent with most modern processes that are holistic and team-oriented. Another problem is that most plans are isolated from the company's business goals; alternatively, organizations should view business results as the ultimate end and the succession plan as a means to that end.

Part 2: The ultimate goal of succession planning is to achieve business results, and teams, rather than individuals, will bring about these results. Thus, the goal of succession-planners should be to build and maintain team continuity to help achieve business results. The plan should also be tailored to the specific needs of the company. Succession planning should be implemented in phases; this makes the program more manageable, open to feedback, and easier to fine-tune. Proposed phases are: (1) Introduce the plan; (2) collect initial data; (3) analyze and provide feedback; (4) implement business strategies; and (5) review and build. Management must be responsible for the plan at all times, and the human resources function should provide support, expertise, and tools for succession planning.

Part 3: The keys to successful data collection are "reduction, consolidation, and automation." In addition to collecting data on individual positions and people, it is important to incorporate information on the team. Both individual and team strengths and weaknesses should be assessed with respect to the business strategy. The succession plan should also be linked to other human-resources systems including training and development, compensation and benefits, EEO and affirmative action, career planning, recruiting, and outplacement.

Charles Borwick. Eight ways to assess succession plans. *HRMagazine,* 38:5, 1993, pp. 109-114.

Borwick offers the following eight steps to improve succession plans: (1) Link the succession plan closely to the business plan. (2) Avoid viewing succession planning as an end in itself; instead focus on continuously improving the process. (3) The process should be "top-down/bottom-up/top-down": initiated at request of senior management and carried out from bottom up; changes to plans or their approval should be communicated from the top down. However, in most succession plans the last part of the top-down cycle is missing. (4) Although succession planning typically has been secretive, companies should talk openly about candidates and involve candidates for whom plans are being made. (5) A succession plan should contain a time frame; this ensures that plans are actually implemented. (6) The more management layers there are in the planning process, the less effective the succession plan will be; therefore, decision making should be pushed down the line and closer to the business context. (7) The review process should seek problems, not pat answers: Instead of just completing prefabricated forms, such as backup charts and employee profiles, managers should also be encouraged to think of problems and important issues to discuss during the review meeting. (8) Avoid massive data collection because this places an unnecessary burden on the organization; collect only pertinent information.

Victoria J. Brush and Ren Nardoni. Integrated data supports AT&T's succession planning. *Personnel Journal,* 71:9, September 1992, pp. 103-109.

The authors describe the basic features and advantages of AT&T's microcomputer-based succession-planning system. The primary advantages of the system are: It has an extensive data capacity; it is a highly versatile system that can grow and change in response to the changing needs of management; it links the succession-planning system with other human-resources information systems such as leadership-development and career-management systems; it has report-writing capabilities, which quickly provide managers with necessary information in the form of tables, charts, and graphs; and it is easy to use, so no outside support is needed to maintain the system. Authors note that although AT&T had specific requirements that drove the acquisition and customization of their system, there are certain system requirements that most organizations should consider when incorporating a computerized succession-planning system (for instance, data capacity, flexibility, ease of use, and ability to link the plan with other systems).

Marilyn Buckner and Lynn Slavenski. Succession planning. In *Human resources management and development handbook* (2nd ed.). W. R. Tracey, Ed. New York: AMACOM, 1994, pp. 561-575.

The authors contend that succession planning involves identifying and analyzing key positions, assessing candidates against job and personal requirements, and creating individual development plans for potential successors. A succession plan should be developed based on an understanding of the organization's culture and operating environment, and a number of key questions should be answered before designing it. For example: Are business units managed or decentralized? Is there a need for generalists, functional specialists, or both? and What problems is the organization trying to solve?

Four basic succession-planning components are provided: (1) identification of successors; (2) assessment of employee promotability to various positions; (3) high-potential employee development; and (4) employee input. The first is typically a bottom-up approach in which managers at lower levels recommend replacements for their direct reports and possibly themselves. Each higher level of management reviews the recommendations and makes revisions. Usually only critical positions are included; many organizations find the top three management levels in the organization are an appropriate number of positions to include.

With respect to the second component, one of the best formal methods is the assessment center, which has demonstrated a high degree of predictability of employee success at more senior levels. Managers may need training in performance appraisal and assessment in order to identify the most promotable employees as succession candidates.

With respect to the third component, the most comprehensive succession plans integrate identification of high-potentials with succession planning.

With respect to the fourth component, too often succession plans fail to incorporate needs and career interests of employees; however, this information should be obtained from career discussions between manager and employee and by asking employees to list their career interests, qualifications, and willingness to relocate. This information can be used in review meetings and for selection information when openings occur.

The authors suggest that the following are key factors for success: top-management support/link to business strategy; line-management involvement; management discussion and review meetings; linkage to other human-resources programs; putting development at the top of the list; credible human-resources staff leadership; and linkage to strategic staffing. Computerization is helpful but not critical to succession planning.

❖ ❖ ❖

John O. Burdett. Crafting tomorrow's leadership today: A practitioner view of succession and replacement planning. *International Journal of Manpower,* 14:8, 1993, pp. 23-33.

Burdett discusses the approach to succession planning taken by the Lawson Mardon Group (LMG), a multinational packaging firm which has more than forty companies in eight countries. A basic tenet of their succession plan is that positions and job success must be defined in behavioral terms (not just based on job descriptions or generic core competencies). Thus, LMG has defined seven critical dimensions of job success which they refer to as essential characteristics; these characteristics are used for succession planning, recruitment and hiring decisions, and individual career-planning discussions. The advantage of this approach is that the succession-planning process does not stand alone but is only one aspect of their overall human-resources planning.

LMG believes that succession planning should not be viewed as an exclusive activity of human resources professionals and that line management must be involved in the process. To facilitate line ownership, succession planning is part of the annual human-resources review, during which both line management and human resources professionals discuss succession planning and other key issues. To prepare for the meetings, line managers are required to do three things: (1) Define essential characteristics for various leadership roles; (2) repeat the essential characteristics exercise to determine what characteristics, if any, will change in three to five years; and (3) evaluate each manager against these essential characteristics—first, as the position is today and, second, as the position will be in the future. The benefit of this approach is that it moves succession planning from an abstract to a very pragmatic level of discussion. It also focuses on planning how to develop managers for the future. One outcome of the review is individual developmental plans to help bridge competence gaps between employees and succession needs.

Robert S. Burnett and James A. Waters. The action profile: A practical aid to career development and succession planning. *Business Horizons,* May-June 1984, pp. 15-21.

The action profile is a tool that can enhance career development and succession planning by creating an organizational understanding of what it takes to perform high-level jobs. The profile provides "a description, in behavioral terms, of the managerial capacities, skills, and personal qualities required in a particular position. It directs attention to what effective incumbents *do* to produce desired results, in distinction to the results themselves or the personality traits of particular managers" (p. 16).

The major challenge in preparing an action profile is to focus on observable job-related behaviors, similar to the approach taken in developing behaviorally anchored rating scales. The development of this profile requires participation from a wide range of senior managers, and the final product represents a synthesis of their views on what it takes to perform well in a senior position.

The authors caution that the action profile is not meant to be a checklist, because seldom will any individual consistently perform all behaviors described on it. An advantage of this tool is that it stimulates developmental thinking and conversations between bosses and subordinates about career

ıent. In addition, it provides a common metric for assessing potential
ness of candidates for particular positions. The authors provide a
lescription of how an action profile was developed for a senior
position (field vice president) at Alcan Aluminum Ltd.

✜ ✜ ✜

Meagan Butterill. A plan for success. *Management Services,* November 1990,
pp. 20-23.

Butterill outlines four types of succession planning: (1) position recruitment; (2) replacement training; (3) succession planning, pure and simple; and
(4) succession planning linked to career management. The first is the traditional type of succession planning; it is a reactive rather than proactive
system. When a vacancy occurs, it's filled from the outside. Although this
system is simple to run, it results in problems such as high turnover of good
managers, high external recruitment, and protracted open vacancy times.

The second involves keeping a list of backup candidates for most
senior positions. Although this approach is likely to reduce senior-staff
turnover and result in developmental training for some, a drawback is that
many replacement-planning systems are rudimentary, and decisions tend to
be subjective rather than objective.

The third concentrates on fast-track candidates for senior positions and
others with potential; it starts at the top of the organization and works down
through its levels. It also uses annual appraisal with feedback to management
and regular reviews and updates of the succession plan. This results in even
less staff turnover and less external recruitment than before.

The fourth is a full-blown planning process, wherein succession planning acts as a bridge to link career management with human resources planning and corporate strategy. It is described as the ideal approach, and organizations that follow this process are characterized by: "encouraging development generally, giving high priority to self-development, operating a two-way
process of career planning, analyzing skills and competencies needed for the
future, using external recruitment to strengthen areas of weakness, having an
ongoing process of management review, giving all staff opportunity for
advancement, having earned loyalty and low turnover" (p. 21).

The author also describes the *SuccessPlan,* which is a menu-driven
database developed by Borwick International. SuccessPlan helps human
resources professionals with succession planning by integrating various
sources of information, such as organizational charts, succession charts, and

information on individual candidates such as readiness for promotion, training, experience, performance, and tenure.

Joseph P. Carnazza. *Succession/replacement planning: Programs and practices.* Center for Research in Career Development, Columbia University, 1982, 71 pages.

Based on interviews with a representative sample of fifteen companies, the author makes several observations about succession planning:

(1) The larger the company, the more likely it is to have a formal succession program.

(2) Key succession-planning elements are common to all successful plans, such as a set of specific objectives, procedures for nominating and identifying candidates, and policies regarding development. However, these elements vary considerably across companies and are tailored to accommodate the unique needs of each company. There is no one best succession plan; the critical issue is to ensure that the program is best suited to the company's needs and culture.

(3) Companies consistently report that the support of the CEO is the single greatest determinant of the program's success or failure.

(4) Companies tend to use one of the following four strategies for the identification/nomination of succession candidates: (a) crown prince—objective is to identify and nurture a single heir for each position; (b) slate—objective is to develop a small number of qualified candidates available for a vacancy; (c) pool—objective is to develop a reservoir of qualified managers capable of performing any number of jobs; and (d) wave—a combination of crown prince and slate strategy, objective is to choose a single heir from a small reservoir of cohorts, each of whom has been developed and nurtured over several years. There are advantages and disadvantages associated with each of these. Again, one approach is not necessarily the best; a company should choose the strategy best suited to its unique environment.

(5) The essence of succession planning is linking executive potential with essential positions in the organization. An effective program requires both, and a program relying only on lists of high-potentials is incomplete.

(6) There must be a link between succession planning and strategic business planning. Most companies use the status quo rather than strategic business plans to define the essential positions. But assuming that the skills

needed for current positions will be sufficient in the future may prove shortsighted.

(7) Developmental strategies are one of the most important components of an effective succession plan. Developmental plans should be formalized, and there should be a mechanism for ensuring that these plans are implemented—one of the biggest determinants of whether a succession plan will survive.

(8) Companies must recognize that succession planning takes considerable time to become fully effective, perhaps as long as five years.

⁘ ⁘ ⁘

Lourine Anderson Clark and Karen S. Lyness. Succession planning as a strategic activity at Citicorp. In *Advances in applied business strategy* (Vol. 2). L. W. Foster, Ed. Greenwich, CT: JAI Press, 1991, pp. 205-224.

Clark and Lyness show how Citicorp attempts to link succession planning and business strategy by involving the same managers in both processes. Also, the succession-planning process is continually reexamined in order to meet changing business needs. Active participation/commitment at all organizational levels is critical for succession planning: Senior management is responsible for words and actions that say development is a priority; the human resources function is responsible for creating development plans and ensuring that they are executed; line management is responsible for identifying talent, executing the plan, and coaching and providing feedback to high-potentials.

Citicorp generally tries to put high-potentials into jobs for which they are no more than sixty-to-seventy percent qualified. They caution that when thinking about stretch assignments, companies need to differentiate "smart" versus "dumb" risks in order to avoid situations in which a person lacks the specific skills that are essential for success in a particular job.

⁘ ⁘ ⁘

Douglas M. Cowherd. On executive succession: A conversation with Lester B. Korn. *Human Resource Management,* 25:2, 1986, pp. 335-347.

Lester B. Korn, the chairman and CEO of Korn/Ferry International, an international executive-search firm, shares his ideas on succession planning. He argues that the succession process is relatively effective at the middle-management level because you can quantify the necessary managerial charac-teristics; however, at the upper echelon (top five-to-twenty positions), longev-ity, luck, and being in the right place at the right time have played far too important a role.

According to Korn, corporate board members are becoming more involved in management succession, and boards should be actively involved with succession planning for at least the top five-to-seven executive positions. Although selecting and developing executive talent for succession should be the responsibility of line management, human resources managers need to play an active and constructive role. A mistake made by these managers is that they focus too much on the mechanics of succession planning and place too little emphasis on research-based management resource planning and development.

Lynn B. Curtis and Joyce E. A. Russell. *A study of succession planning programs in Fortune 500 firms.* Paper presented at the Eighth Annual Conference of the Society for Industrial and Organizational Psychol-ogy, San Francisco, CA, 1993.

This study found that a majority (seventy percent) of eighty-six U.S. Fortune 500 firms consider succession planning a priority in their firm. Organizations reported using programs both to identify high-potentials as well as to develop them (for example, individual development plans and management-development programs). Respondents indicated that their succession plans were moderately related to the organization's strategic business plan and moderately effective for choosing senior-level managers. They also indicated that succession plans were most successful in promoting white males, moderately successful in advancing women, slightly successful in promoting minorities, and not at all to slightly successful in advancing employees with disabilities.

C. Brooklyn Derr, Candice Jones, and Edmund L. Toomey. Managing high-potential employees: Current practices in thirty-three U.S. corporations. *Human Resource Management*, 27:3, 1988, pp. 272-290.

A survey of thirty-three companies revealed that the three most com-mon stages of managing high-potentials are: (1) identifying and selecting them, (2) developing them, and (3) going through leadership succession. The number of high-potential candidates decreases at each stage. At the first stage, outstanding job performance is typically the criterion used to create a large pool of top performers, who then receive significant test experiences. Those who succeed in their first trial assignments, and demonstrate devotion to the company, proceed to the second stage, wherein they undergo more specific and tailored development. Training at this stage usually includes a two-pronged approach: on-the-job training and classroom instruction. The most commonly used method of on-the-job training is job rotation, which was reported by eighty-four percent of the surveyed companies. Classroom instruction includes both company-sponsored courses (reported by sixty-three percent), and external classroom instruction and executive-development courses (reported by fifty-three percent).

Starting at the end of the second stage and continuing in the third, high-potentials are closely monitored by a management-review committee, which typically includes the CEO. At the beginning of the third stage, the number of high-potentials decreases substantially to a select group of potential successors for top-management jobs.

When queried about obstacles to management of high-potentials, companies reported the following problems: lack of adequate funding for development; limited availability of positions for high-potentials; reluctance of managers to give up their identified high-potentials for developmental assignments; difficulty of defining and measuring potential; and losing high-potentials to competition.

❖ ❖ ❖

Samantha Drake. Succession planning. *Human Resource Executive,* May 1993, pp. 30-31.

Drake describes the succession plans in five organizations.

Royal Bank of Canada: A 360-degree evaluation of managers is used to identify high-potentials for succession planning; these people are then transferred within the company to gain experience or specific training.

Merck & Co. Inc.: Mobility within the business is the key to development of high-potentials.

PepsiCo: About 6,000 salaried employees go through a process of performance planning appraisal/developmental feedback with their supervisors, from which a profile of the person's developmental needs, strengths, and career plans is constructed. Development includes additional training and special assignments, such as start-ups and working on committees. Line management is actively involved in the succession-planning process.

Hershey Foods Corp.: Managers compile profiles of high-growth individuals, and five-year development plans are made. Development involves lateral movements or promotions to another division. Separate lists for women and minorities are generated; these lists include individuals who are not currently part of the organization's succession plan but who have demonstrated potential.

Kmart Co.: Individual development plans incorporate the employee's career goals and include lateral movements and possible promotions. Assigning a mentor is sometimes included as part of the developmental plan. High-potential assistant store managers who have been with Kmart for three to four years are assigned to work with an executive at corporate headquarters for eighteen to twenty-four months.

Executive Knowledgeworks. *Succession planning in America's corporations: How 64 top companies prepare for the future.* Palatine, IL: Anthony J. Fresina & Associates, Inc., 1988, 65 pages.

This report describes the results of in-depth telephone interviews with representatives from sixty-four U.S. corporations. Specific approaches to succession planning vary, but a successful process consists of four basic elements. There does not appear to be a good or bad way of applying them, but effective systems seem to address each in some way:

(1) Gather information on managerial job requirements for the company as a whole and for specific jobs. These requirements should be defined at the general strategic level (for instance, What kind of managers will we need in the future?) and at the specific job level (that is, identifying specific job criteria for each position covered by the plan). Data on specific job requirements and demands should be collected, for instance, through job analysis or action profiles.

(2) Gather information on candidates for managerial positions. Ninety-five percent of the surveyed companies reported formal evaluation of candidates, and this process is usually tied to the performance-appraisal system. In addition to assessing performance, potential for growth should be considered.

(3) Develop plans for those who might fill particular positions and develop plans for how people will be prepared to fill these positions. There is no magic formula for completing this phase; the critical element is the review.

There may be several reviews; some organizations conduct them at the department, division, and corporate levels, the results of each serving as input for the next higher level. Or there may be only one review, in which a few of the very senior executives participate. The most commonly reported methods for preparing people for particular positions were: early practical leadership experience, cross-functional training, task-force assignments, line/staff switch, and corporate assignments.

(4) Implement succession plans and development plans. The key to implementing the succession plan is understanding that it is a management function, not a staff responsibility. There is widespread agreement that succession-planning efforts are not likely to succeed unless top management is heavily committed and involved and unless responsibility for the process lies with line management rather than within a staff function. "The staff's role is to serve as internal consultant, advising line management and providing whatever programs or services they need, but not to serve as the driving force behind the effort" (p. 52). However, only twenty-two percent of the respondents cited line management when asked who was responsible for succession planning in their organizations; in contrast, seventy-eight percent said overall responsibility resides with the human resources function.

The report also includes a sample of succession-planning materials from companies that participated in the study.

❖ ❖ ❖

Julie A. Fenwick-Magrath. Executive development: Key factors for success. *Personnel,* 65:7, July 1988, pp. 68-72.

The author reports the results of a survey of representatives from twelve companies considered to be "state-of-the-art" organizations in executive development. In their responses, a majority of the survey participants agreed that there are five characteristics of effective executive-development programs: (1) extensive and visible involvement by the CEO; (2) a clearly articulated and understood executive-development philosophy and strategy, which is tailored to the company's unique history, culture, environment, and business needs; (3) executive-development policies and strategies that are directly linked to the corporation's business strategy; (4) a bottom-up succession-planning process (that is, the process begins in the division and functional areas), which includes planned on-the-job developmental assignments and executive educational programs; and (5) line owns the process; staff supports it.

On-the-job development was reported to be the single most effective, albeit underutilized, developmental tool. The four types of experiences that were most often used and most effective were task forces, job rotations, overseas assignments, and temporary assignments of relatively short duration.

✣ ✣ ✣

Stewart D. Friedman. Succession systems in large corporations: Characteristics and correlates of performance. *Human Resource Management,* 25:2, 1986, pp. 191-213.

Friedman surveyed 235 Fortune 500 firms to assess how the following seven dimensions of succession systems relate to corporate reputation and financial performance: (1) Formalization—the extent to which written rules and procedures exist for succession planning; (2) Control Systems—checks and balances; (3) Resource Allocation—the extent to which time and energy are devoted to succession planning; (4) Information Systems—the extent to which data are gathered from relevant sources and used during succession planning; (5) Political Criteria—the extent to which selection decisions are based on loyalty, network ties, and other nonability factors; (6) Technical Criteria—the extent to which selection decisions are based on past performance, range of experience, and other ability factors; and (7) Staff Role—the extent to which human resources professionals are involved in and take ownership of succession planning.

Correlational results are presented. There was no relationship between Formalization and organizational performance, which suggests that Formalization "may be a necessary but not sufficient condition for effective succession systems." Political Criteria was positively related to organizational performance, which supports the importance of hiring from within. The remaining succession-system dimensions were positively related to performance, with the exception of Staff Role, where there were both positive and negative relationships. Staff credibility and access to needed information were positively related to organizational performance, whereas staff ownership of succession issues (that is, less line ownership) was associated with lower performance. These findings suggest that the succession staff should be involved but that responsibility must remain with line management.

The author included these suggestions for effective succession planning: Link the plan with the business strategy; ensure active involvement of the CEO; evaluate and compensate executives for their efforts to develop

their subordinates; and focus more on the long-term benefits of using placements as developmental opportunities.

Stewart D. Friedman. Succession systems in the public sector: Lessons from
the Oklahoma Department of Corrections. *Public Personnel Management,* 19:3, 1990, pp. 291-303.

Oklahoma's Department of Corrections (DOC) is presented as an
example of effective succession planning in the public sector. If possible,
candidates for key positions are promoted from within, and movement of
people across divisional lines is favored because such moves are developmental. As part of the selection process for middle- to high-level positions,
candidates are involved in intensive interviews where they get feedback and
are counseled with respect to how they can strengthen their skills and abilities
to become better candidates. Once an upper-level executive assumes a new
position, he or she embarks on a "learning journey." For a period of two-to-
three weeks, the newly assigned manager conducts no work other than
participating in extensive interviews and discussions with key people
throughout the DOC. These journeys help the manager build network ties,
gain insight into the workings of the agency, and identify sources of support.

Stewart D. Friedman and Theodore P. LeVino. Strategic appraisal and development at General Electric Company. In *Strategic human resource
management.* C. J. Fombrun, N. M. Tichy, & M. A. Devanna, Eds. New
York: John Wiley & Sons, 1984, pp. 183-201.

The General Electric Company holds executives accountable for the
development of managerial talent, and people performance is a factor when
bonuses are determined. Executive Management Staff (EMS) is responsible
for management development at GE. EMS has three majors sets of activities:
The Slate System, Organization and Staffing Reviews (O&S Reviews), and
Accomplishment Analyses.
    The Slate System requires that an executive with an opening in the top
600 positions get a candidate slate from EMS and select from it. This slate is
the basis for corporate control over the quality of staffing and executive
development and is based on knowledge of the job specifications, who would
best contribute to the job, and who would most benefit from the experience.

O&S Reviews are held by the Corporate Executive Office to look at executive talent in the company. The process begins with department-level managers discussing with each of their subordinates their developmental needs based on career interests and strengths and weaknesses, and so on. (It is important to note that this is not linked to compensation decisions.) The manager submits a succession plan for the manager and his or her staff. This information is then presented to the manager's superior in the O&S meeting, and the data are added to the EMS inventory.

Accomplishment Analysis is the most concentrated data-gathering component of EMS. An EMC (executive-management consultant) interviews a manager for three-to-four hours, holds a two-to-three hour meeting with the person's boss, and may interview former associates and subordinates. A written summary of the individual's achievements, possible developmental plans, and so forth is the outcome of this assessment and becomes part of the EMS file on the manager.

❖ ❖ ❖

Cheryl Getty. Planning successfully for succession planning. *Training and Development,* 47:11, 1993, pp. 31-33.

Getty asserts that there are four critical challenges for succession planning.

(1) Lifting the cloak: Most succession programs have been "cloaked in secrecy" and involve only a few human-resources development specialists and top executives. However, managers who are unaware of succession plans may not provide selected candidates with important developmental opportunities and feedback. A more propitious strategy would be a bottom-up process, which encourages participation from a larger group of managers.

(2) Broadening views: Organizations with separate functions or business units often develop a narrow view of where desirable talent can be found and, consequently, ignore employees in some units and do not broaden employees by rotating them across different functions or businesses. To avoid this, succession plans should be presented in a group format, wherein the organization's top managers give their proposed succession plans for their individual units. This way, managers learn about talent outside of their areas as well as staffing needs and developmental opportunities that exist across the organization.

(3) Filling in the "black hole": Many managers complain that they do not get feedback after they submit succession plans and, therefore, become

hesitant to implement development activities for their employees. Hence, the need for feedback.

(4) Using succession plans: Organizations need to treat succession plans as "living documents."

✤ ✤ ✤

Lynda Gratton and Michael Syrett. Heirs apparent: Succession strategies for the future. *Personnel Management,* 22:1, 1990, pp. 34-38.

The authors describe four different, but equally successful, approaches to succession planning at IBM, Amstrad, BAT, and Hanson. Differences among these programs are used to demonstrate that there is no one universal approach to succession planning. Rather, effective companies match their succession strategies to their business strategies. At IBM, for instance, talent is identified early on, and succession planning involves a series of planned job moves that provide both cross-functional and international experience. In contrast, at Amstrad, which is a younger and fast-growing corporation, succession processes are more ad hoc and subject to revision.

The authors caution that companies "cannot simply impose the best practices of the most successful companies in an indiscriminate manner," and it is increasingly important that programs be flexible and linked to future requirements. In addition, succession plans should be based more on the needs of the individual rather than exclusively on organizational needs and requirements of the job.

✤ ✤ ✤

Douglas T. Hall. Human resource development and organizational effectiveness. In *Strategic human resource management.* C. J. Fombrun, N. M.
Tichy, & M. A. Devanna, Eds. New York: John Wiley & Sons, 1984,
pp. 159-181.

As a way to link succession planning with business strategy, Hall proposes employing *strategic human-resource development*—that is, the "identification of needed skills and active management of employee learning for the long-range future in relation to explicit corporate and business strategies" (p. 159). He asserts that developmental efforts often fail because the critical link between development and organizational strategy is missing. In addition, the time span of developmental activities is often too short, and the focus is frequently on skill requirements in a new or present assignment rather than on requirements for the future.

Four outcomes of development are: performance and attitudes (short-term outcomes) and adaptability and identity (long-term outcomes). The problem is that most organizations rely on formal, classroom approaches to development and focus on developing short-term, task-related skills (that is, performance). Too seldom are attitudes, adaptability, and identity the focus of developmental plans; interventions for these outcomes include environment-based activities, such as job rotations, cross-functional moves, task forces, project teams, and consulting or troubleshooting assignments.

Policies that support development include: establishing a clear organizational commitment to the development of internal candidates for job openings, linking the manager's career development with the subordinate's, and ensuring participation of top management in the process.

✣ ✣ ✣

Douglas T. Hall. Dilemmas in linking succession planning to individual executive learning. *Human Resource Management,* 25:2, 1986, pp. 235-265.

In this article, Hall discusses some of the pitfalls of succession planning and two types of executive learning and offers suggestions for improvement.

The pitfalls of succession planning are: (1) Succession planning is divorced from business strategy. (2) Top executives tend to choose successors very much like themselves rather than identify managers with different profiles of skills and experiences that will be needed for the future (homosocial reproduction). (3) Top executives focus their efforts on identifying high-potentials and fail to put enough emphasis on the process of development. (4) There is insufficient follow-up on developmental activities. (5) Succession plans are treated as confidential, and organizations rarely consider a person's willingness to assume a position or to engage in developmental plans. (6) Succession planning can actually result in anti-developmental consequences. Managers who realize that they are on the fast track will play it safe, take fewer risks, and consequently avoid activities that lead to learning; in contrast, so-called solid citizens, who realize that they are not on the fast track, will be unmotivated to learn. (7) Many succession plans result in executive immaturity. High-potentials feel that the organization is plotting a career path for them and fail to take personal responsibility for their development.

There are two types of executive learning. Task learning is "improving the knowledge, skills, and abilities necessary to perform higher level jobs effectively" (p. 245). Personal learning is "the mastery of the socioemotional tasks associated with the person's stage of life." These two types of learning relate to four career outcomes. Task learning results in improved performance in the short-term and adaptability in the long-term. Personal learning in the short-term helps executives develop career and life attitudes, and in the long term contributes to developing one's sense of identity. Although most work on executive development has focused on task learning and short-term issues of improved performance, there should be more emphasis on long-term learning and personal learning.

Hall offers suggestions on how to improve succession planning and executive learning: (1) Think through the link between the organization's basic objectives and the skills that top executives will need in the future. (2) Increase the priority and preparation of development plans. (3) Encourage active learning for executives. (4) Design learning seminars for corporate officers. (5) Integrate succession and career planning, and involve the candidate—perhaps the greatest need of all. (6) Eliminate fast tracks; create developmental environments and candidate pools. "Rather than selecting high-potential candidates first and then developing them, we are more likely to experience success if we develop first and then select." (7) Create diversity and learning opportunities throughout the career. (8) Capitalize on natural learning opportunities provided in the everyday organizational environment.

❖ ❖ ❖

Douglas T. Hall. How top management and the organization itself can block
    effective executive succession. *Human Resource Management,* 28:1,
    1989, pp. 5-24.

Hall asserts that the most critical component of succession planning is at the top (the strategic level). Yet most organizations focus attention on the implementation level (programs and systems) without first getting agreement on the necessary human-resources strategy and policies. Only after top management has agreed on and articulated the necessary policies should work proceed to the design and implementation of specific systems and programs.

Examples of policies that support executive succession and development are: promotion from within; policies favoring lateral, cross-functional, or cross-business movement; and linking subordinate development to managers' rewards. The increasingly limited availability of key positions for high-potentials requires organizations to create developmental opportunities, such as projects, task forces, and temporary assignments.

Douglas T. Hall and Fred K. Foulkes. Senior executive development as a competitive advantage. In *Advances in applied business strategy*. L. W. Foster, Ed. Greenwich, CT: JAI Press, 1990, pp. 183-203.

The authors conducted a three-year study of practices in companies with a reputation for effective executive continuity and succession planning. They identified seven myths and challenges associated with succession planning:

(1) Although essential, the link between succession planning and corporate strategy is absent in most organizations.

(2) Although succession planning traditionally has been viewed as a corporate-level activity in which candidates are groomed for high-level corporate positions, decentralization of business units has resulted in a shift from "corporate property" to "business unit property": Business units focus on developing their own talent and there are few incentives for sharing talent across business and functions.

(3) Although the assumption is that succession planning increases bench strength and promotes executive continuity, it is equally important that the company possess human resources policies and organizational designs that support effective succession planning.

(4) Although a strength of many companies in the past was promotion-from-within policies, many companies today are rethinking their strict adherence to these policies (for example, the need to be globally competitive sometimes means looking outside for talent).

(5) Although the involvement of top-level management is essential for effective succession planning, an "unfortunate by-product of involving top management" is that they tend to produce people similar to themselves, which does not necessarily guarantee the identification and development of strong candidates. Thus, an important succession-planning challenge is to overcome executive cloning.

(6) Although it's often assumed that succession planning and executive development are linked, in most organizations these two systems are weakly connected, and techniques for the assessment of talent are much more sophisticated than developmental techniques.

(7) Because the business environment and knowledge, skills, and abilities required for executive positions are changing so rapidly, executives of the future increasingly will need to be "self-learners."

Obstacles to effective succession planning include decentralization, which has made cross-business and cross-functional developmental moves more difficult. Also, downsizing and delayering have eliminated promotional opportunities traditionally slated for high-potentials.

Two case studies are used to illustrate how succession planning works for two different types of companies: (1) those with a relatively focused business strategy and (2) those with a more diverse strategy and relatively autonomous business units. Keys to success include CEO involvement and a reward system that recognizes executives for the development of managers. The emphasis of succession planning should not be solely on technical and operational details. For organizations with a weak human-resources function or limited top-management involvement, the board of directors should be actively involved with succession planning.

❖ ❖ ❖

Douglas T. Hall and Kent W. Seibert. Strategic management development: Linking organizational strategy, succession planning, and managerial learning. In *Career development: Theory and practice.* D. H. Montross & C. J. Shinkman, Eds. Springfield, IL: Charles C. Thomas, 1991, pp. 255-275.

The authors suggest that succession planning should be linked to both the future direction of the organization and the learning and development of managers; but these links rarely exist. Current succession-planning activities are categorized and their problems are described.

(1) A one-shot staffing decision is a reactive activity, which involves finding the best-qualified individual to fill a vacant position; little attention is given to development.

(2) Replacement planning is a more proactive approach; planning is done for a large number of positions on a regular schedule. A drawback is that objective criteria (for example, job descriptions) are typically not used.

(3) Succession planning involves focusing on both positions and candidates; there's an assessment process, which results in development plans for high-potentials. The problem is that there is more emphasis on assessment than on development and follow-up. As an alternative, authors propose strategic management development, which focuses on anticipated future

management positions, expected skill requirements of those positions, and developing people for those positions.

Hall and Seibert also provide a model of managerial learning and development (p. 264), which suggests that managers bring important inputs to their managerial position: life stage, career stage, career anchor, learning style, gender, and personality. Managerial learning is also affected by where one is in the management hierarchy. Four classes of skills that can be acquired through managerial learning are technical skills, human skills, conceptual skills, and intrapersonal skills. These skills, in turn, result in both short-term and long-term career outcomes.

Richard Hansen and Richard H. Wexler. Effective succession planning. *Employment Relations Today,* 15:1, Spring 1988, pp. 19-24.

The authors outline the basic steps involved in developing a succession plan. An example of how one organization has successfully implemented the succession-planning process is also provided. Clearly defining the objectives of the succession plan is the first critical step, and these objectives should be in line with the organization's business plans and relevant to the needs of the organization.

Succession planning is accomplished by clearly defining the needs for particular positions and planning how to effectively develop people to meet those needs. Merely having lists of potential candidates without understanding current and future job needs will render a succession-planning program ineffective. To be effective, it should also be designed to respond to the evolving needs of the organization. However, there is often the tendency for elements of the program to become fixed, and the authors argue that "one sure measure of an ineffective system is that it does not change over time." Individuals should be reminded that the ultimate responsibility for development lies with themselves first and the organization second.

S. Robert Hernandez, Cynthia Carter Haddock, William M. Behrendt, and
    Walter F. Klein. Management development and succession planning:
    Lessons for health service organizations. *Journal of Management
    Development,* 10:4, 1991, pp. 19-30.

The philosophy and structure of a succession-planning/management-development system that was designed for Barnes Hospital in St. Louis, Missouri, is described. The process consists of two separate but complementary components—the performance-appraisal process and the developmental review—which are performed at different times of the year. The separation of these functions makes developmental discussions less threatening and more productive for employees, because compensation is not involved.

In contrast to the performance appraisal, which focuses on the evaluation of past performance, the developmental review relies on individual development plans (IDPs) and focuses on potential for future growth. The IDP focuses on eleven management characteristics that were specifically identified as important for the success of future managers at Barnes. Each manager is rated by two supervisors on these eleven characteristics; once their developmental needs (that is, characteristics with low ratings) have been identified, actions are planned to help develop the specific characteristics that need improvement. A developmental review and career discussion between each manager and his or her supervisor is also conducted. These meetings have been useful, because managers have found that each of their subordinates have very distinct developmental needs and career aspirations.

The authors also offer the following requisites for succession planning: "(1) commitment of senior management; (2) adequate staff support; (3) linkage of succession planning with other human-resources systems and planning activities; (4) adequate human-resources information system; (5) organization structure and job design, which facilitate experiential learning; (6) commitment to promotion from within; (7) training for line managers who will implement the program; (8) clear accountabilities for implementation of development plans; (9) inclusion of multiple individuals in the assessment/identification process; and (10) periodic evaluation of the program" (p. 28).

John R. Hinrichs and George P. Hollenbeck. Leadership development.
In *Developing human resources* (Vol. 5). K. W. Wexley, Ed.
Washington, DC: Bureau of National Affairs, 1990, pp. 221-258.

The authors provide seventeen imperatives for successful executive/
management development, derived from their reading of the literature and
conversations with executives from major corporations: (1) Adopt a long-
term view of development. (2) Emphasize the importance of quality selection
decisions, because development begins with who is hired. (3) Identify talent
early, with an early bias toward selecting several rather than too few high-
potentials. (4) Give high-potentials growth opportunities and special experiences. (5) Focus on and reward high performance, because this encourages
development. (6) Emphasize human assets as part of the business strategy.
(7) Emphasize growth and development for all employees. (8) Focus on the
short-term while also being future-oriented. (9) Make an effort to create
developmental job assignments when few job openings or opportunities are
available. (10) Tie development to critical career transitions, such as staff-to-
line switches. (11) Evaluate and reward managers for their efforts to develop
talent; include mentoring as part of development. (12) Continuously assess
employee performance and potential using many observers and various tools.
(13) Use job rotations and special assignments not only for functional reasons
but also as stretch assignments with developmental opportunities. (14) Rely
on diverse developmental methods, because the odds of development increase
by providing a range of experiences. (15) Ensure that there is CEO and top-
management commitment and support for development. (16) Ensure that
development programs are driven by line management and not seen as owned
by the human resources function. (17) Provide corporate support for development, but also view development as the responsibility of the individual. The
second half of the chapter provides a case study which demonstrates these
imperatives.

Idalene F. Kesner. Succession planning. *Credit,* 15, 1989, pp. 29-35.

Kesner asserts that succession planning is most successful when pre-
ceded by a general strategic-planning process which includes the following
five steps: (1) Determine the organization's mission and objectives.
(2) Assess the organization's external environment. (3) Assess the
organization's internal environment (that is, identify strengths and weak-

nesses on a function-by-function basis). (4) Identify and evaluate strategic alternatives. (5) Choose and implement the best strategy.

Where does succession planning fit into strategic planning and who is responsible? The answer depends on the managerial level under consideration. In the case of CEO succession, responsibility lies with the board of directors, and succession planning is typically introduced at the end of the third step. At the level just below the CEO, key decision-makers often include the CEO, the current incumbent of the position, and other VPs; planning tends to be introduced later in the stage, typically at the end of the fourth step. At the middle-management levels, succession planning is usually handled by a divisional VP and occurs at the end of the fifth step.

✛ ✛ ✛

Diana Kramer. Executive succession and development systems: A practical
    approach. In *Human resource forecasting and strategy development:*
    Guidelines for analyzing and fulfilling organizational needs.
    M. London, E. S. Bassman, & J. P. Fernandez, Eds. Westport, CT:
    Quorum Books, 1990, pp. 99-112.

The author proposes a ten-step approach to executive succession and development planning: (1) Conduct a needs analysis. (2) Focus needs analysis on a pilot group. (3) Check the needs analysis and verify its accuracy. (4) Integrate executive succession planning with other human resources programs. (5) Conduct a job analysis. (6) Draft a process and review with line managers. (7) Provide training on program procedures. (8) Make sure there is implementation. (9) Provide administrative support for the system. (10) Establish the evaluation system.

Kramer places particular emphasis on the following: Ensure line ownership of the process; use a job analysis to identify objective behavioral dimensions on which potential successors can be evaluated; integrate the succession plan with the business plan and other human-resources systems; and develop people.

✛ ✛ ✛

Chris Lee. Identifying and developing the next generation of managers.
    Training, October 1981, pp. 36-39.

High-potential individuals are no longer willing to let their organizations manage their careers, and succession plans must take individual desires into account. Lee asserts that allowing employees to take responsibility for their own career planning and development is the key to an effective succession plan.

There are a variety of succession plans, but successful plans typically include the following elements: (1) integration with overall strategic planning, which forecasts future management needs; (2) an objective evaluation of an employee's current performance, skills, and potential; (3) periodic reviews to ensure that succession plans do not become outdated; (4) development programs; and (5) visible support of top management.

Michael S. Leibman and Ruth A. Bruer. Where there's a will there's a way. *Journal of Business Strategy,* 15:2, March/April 1994, pp. 26-34.

The authors discuss challenges of succession planning and provide examples of companies that have successfully met these challenges. The challenges include such factors as the fact that the nature of succession planning is changing; the traditional approach of placing the right person in the right job at the right time is outdated. The "magic formula" for succession planning is that it should be "an ongoing process like the business planning itself" (p. 28). Also, the dominant role of teams in organizations indicates that succession planning should involve planning how to prepare not just individuals but teams of people who will be capable of taking over the duties of a position. "Instead of identifying the right person for the right position at the right time, corporations are looking to continually develop strong leadership teams for strategic tasks" (p. 29). In fact, the authors argue that the growing importance of teams has diminished the utility of succession planning which focuses on the individual.

CEO involvement in the process is essential, because it's only through the CEO that the necessary linkage of people and business can take place. Succession planning must be a line-driven process; Corning and Weyerhaeuser are given as examples of how to ensure line ownership. Having the same executives sit in on both management-development reviews and strategic-planning meetings improves succession planning.

Walter R. Mahler. Management succession planning: New approaches for the
  80's. *Human Resource Planning,* 4:4, 1981, pp. 221-227.

Mahler proposes several ways to improve succession planning. First,
the program should be designed to meet the specific needs of the organization. For example, the succession plan should be different for a company that
is in a rapid-growth mode, versus one that is characterized by slow growth or
decline. Also, different business strategies will require different types of
managerial abilities and, therefore, require different succession plans. Second,
better evaluative data, such as General Electric's Accomplishment Analysis,
are needed. Third, the annual human-resources review process must be made
more productive by ensuring that executives have thorough discussions about
organizational needs and talent, that they develop specific plans of action, and
that they implement these plans as well. The author's experience with conducting workshops on management-succession planning has shown that
tutoring executives in their preparation for the review can improve the quality
of the process. Fourth, the management-succession plan should complement
the strategic business plan. Fifth, succession planning should be a collaborative planning process which meets both organizational and individual needs.

❖ ❖ ❖

Walter R. Mahler and Steven J. Drotter. *The succession planning handbook
  for the chief executive.* Midland Park, NJ: Mahler Publishing Co., 1986,
  170 pages.

Based on their experience with succession plans in a variety of organizations, the authors propose ten major requirements for succession planning,
and a chapter is devoted to each.
    (1) Define the purpose and philosophy of the succession plan (chapter
2): The "Achilles' heel" of most succession plans is that they lack purpose
and philosophy. Defining the purpose increases the likelihood that priority
will be given to the succession plan and makes the plan more oriented toward
achieving end results. A caveat is that borrowing programs is dangerous, and
it is better to have a program tailored to specific organizational purposes.
    (2) Top-management action (chapter 3): Top management must make a
commitment to and participate actively in the succession-planning process.
    (3) Professional staff contribution (chapter 4): Staff's role should be
that of catalyst, which implies "actively interacting, stimulating, and pushing

the process along, while still keeping neutral in the process" (p. 29). Staff should avoid creating the perception that it rules the process.

(4) The human resources review (chapter 5): This process, in which executives meet to discuss the performance, promotability, and developmental needs of management, should be considered the most important aspect of the entire planning process. Basic questions and issues to be covered during this review process include the business plan, organizational structure and changes, performance evaluations, promotability forecasts, developmental plans, special programs (for instance, affirmative action), and quarterly-action schedule (that is, the specific actions that will be taken each quarter of the year).

Major pitfalls associated with current human-resources reviews are: (a) the lack of interest and involvement by the CEO; (b) the mechanics of the process are carried out but results are not forthcoming; (c) the review process is viewed by line managers as owned by the human resources function; (d) the review process becomes too complex; (e) the quality of preparation for review is low; (f) there is an absence of follow-through on the plans resulting from the review; (g) the initial design of the review process is not improved periodically; (h) several obsolete practices are still used; (i) one or more bias tendencies subvert the review process (for instance, preference for individuals under the age of forty); (j) there is an absence of effective discussion during the review process; (k) replacement nominations are accepted at face value without adequate consideration of evaluative data; (l) adverse environmental factors (for instance, bonus plans which focus on short-term financial results) are overlooked.

(5) Helpful data system (chapter 6): There must be good accurate information, which is up-to-date and readily available. Career-aspiration data for succession candidates should also be included as important data.

(6) Selection on corporate-wide basis (chapter 7): Companies "must not only develop talent but make proper use of the talent," because quality selection decisions are closely linked to the effectiveness of a succession plan.

(7) Development of future high-level managers (chapter 8): The authors propose emphasizing challenging job experiences as one way to improve current developmental efforts, though they caution that short-tenure developmental moves often prove disastrous, and a manager should stay in a given challenging work situation for at least three-to-four years.

(8) Getting results from an investment in management education (chapter 9): Educational programs often fail because management assumes

that these programs will do the entire job of development and, consequently, they neglect other key aspects of development. Suggestions for improvement include developing educational programs that are tailored to very specific outcomes, using line managers to provide internal education, and getting executives to realize that learning is continuous and extends beyond the classroom.

(9) Getting a developmental contribution from an objectives program (chapter 11): In place of performance appraisal, individuals should be given more control over the process by preparing their own performance objectives, which they can use to monitor and assess their own progress and developmental needs.

(10) Integration of succession planning with other management programs (chapter 12): Even the best-designed succession plan will not produce results if it is at odds with other management programs. For example, succession plans often fail to reflect the human resources implications of business strategy, and financial incentives reward executives for short-term results rather than long-term developmental efforts (although many companies are now including "development of managers" in their bonus plans).

Chapter 13 discusses three special succession-planning challenges: maintaining a constant people flow, incorporating affirmative action into succession plans, and keys to successful expatriate job assignments. Chapter 14 addresses succession planning in a large diversified company, and chapter 15 addresses succession planning in small organizations.

Walter R. Mahler and Frank Gaines. *Succession planning in leading companies.* Midland Park, NJ: Mahler Publishing Co., 1983, 167 pages.

This book provides guidelines for effective succession planning. The authors' basic premise is that the most important process in an organization's overall succession program is the executive review. They discuss how to make this process more effective and how to avoid its pitfalls. Included in the appendix are several examples of succession-planning documents used by companies such as IBM, General Electric, and Exxon.

Mahler and Gaines' four general recommendations are: (1) Establish the right purpose or outcomes of the program. (2) Carefully decide on the content; this should involve thinking about the business plan, organizational structure, performance evaluations, promotability forecasts, future plans, and individual development plans. (3) Establish a thorough process; it should be a bottom-up process and not restricted to top levels of management. (4) Provide follow-up; ensure that planned actions are actually taken by generating a list of specific actions and specifying time frames for these actions. Make specific outcomes of the succession plan visible (for instance, an annual report that summarizes the succession plan's progress and outcomes).

The executive review should result in individual development plans, which focus on three types of action (in order of importance): (1) a plan for developmental work experiences and assignments; (2) a plan for coaching by a superior, who will help the person with his or her specific developmental needs; and (3) a plan for an educational course or program.

The succession plan should be an "evolving and iterative process," and any significant changes in the strategic plan must be reflected in the succession plan. In spite of the problems associated with performance appraisal (such as rater biases), it should be a critical component of the succession-planning process.

In order to overcome the difficult task of adequately defining potential, the authors recommend using promotability forecasts. This requires identifying key challenges of a given position and pointing out specifications; then candidates are identified who should be able to meet the specifications within a given time frame.

✥ ✥ ✥

Morgan W. McCall. Executive development as a business strategy. *The Journal of Business Strategy,* 13:1, January/February 1992, pp. 25-31.

McCall asserts that executive development must be one of the top five corporate priorities. Four fundamental issues must be addressed for executive-development efforts to succeed.

(1) Identify talent/potential: This should focus not on whether people possess the desired qualities now but on whether candidates have abilities that will enable them to acquire the desired end-state qualities through developmental experiences.

(2) Match talent and opportunity: Relying on the immediate manager to ensure that those with potential are given appropriate developmental opportunities is a questionable method, and more sophisticated systems such as succession planning are better for assessing potential and tracking talented people over time.

(3) Provide opportunities that help develop leadership skills: The best practices in executive development systematically use experience for devel-

opmental opportunities. Exposure to new challenges (for instance, job rotations, special assignments, projects, and task forces) stretches a person beyond his or her current abilities and provides an important opportunity for on-the-job development. Organizations should avoid placing candidates into assignments only when they are ready or fully qualified, because the development of new skills requires that a person not already possess the skills required for the position (that is, that the person be stretched). Critical to the success of these learning opportunities is the identification of what it is that one specifically hopes to learn from an experience.

(4) Facilitate learning from experience: A developmentally oriented organization does not just "throw talented people into fires"; rather, it provides catalysts that facilitate and maximize individual learning from experience. Examples of such catalysts include setting developmental goals, establishing accountability for attaining them, providing necessary resources, providing regular feedback on developmental progress, and coaching. Such catalysts, however, are frequently missing from developmental activities.

❖ ❖ ❖

Cynthia D. McCauley, Lorrina J. Eastman, and Patricia J. Ohlott. Linking management selection and development through stretch assignments. *Human Resource Management,* 34:1, Winter 1995, pp. 93-115.

The authors describe managerial jobs in terms of fifteen qualitatively and empirically derived developmental components. They represent features of jobs which challenge managers and therefore provide opportunities for on-the-job learning (examples include reduction decisions; transitions, such as moving from one functional area to another; and dealing with adverse business conditions). Understanding these components helps decision-makers effectively incorporate management-development considerations into selection processes.

When selecting an individual for a position, decision-makers should seek a good match between the candidate's competencies and demands of the job. At the same time, though, they should assess how much stretch the assignment will provide; when a job stretches a manager beyond his or her current abilities, it provides important opportunities for learning and development.

The authors address concerns associated with incorporating developmental considerations in selection issues. One example is how to assess the extent of various developmental components in a particular job and how to find the right fit or balance between a manager's talents and demands of the job so that the job offers learning opportunities but the stretch is not overwhelming.

In addition, they discuss how the developmental-component framework can enhance the developmental emphasis of succession-planning systems. For example, the framework could help organizations create assignments, such as special projects and cross-functional moves for high-potentials.

James E. McElwain. Succession plans designed to manage change. *HR Magazine,* 36:2, 1991, pp. 67-71.

McElwain, vice president of personnel resources at NCR Corporation (now AT&T Global Information Solutions), discusses his company's succession-planning system—what works and why. The author contends that any good succession process must include: "(1) a systematic rather than anecdotal way of identifying candidates; (2) cross-divisional sharing of people and information; (3) leadership that rewards managers for promoting (rather than holding onto) their best employees; (4) career paths that move not just up a specialized ladder but across the company; (5) frequent opportunities for employees to accept new challenges; and (6) recognition that employees have a stake in the company and share its successes" (p. 67).

One of the greatest failings of many succession plans is the "crown prince" syndrome: Management fails to identify all the best candidates, and those considered for advancement are simply those who have become visible to them. Another problem is that too much information is needed to track everyone; the author suggests that computerizing such an intense information-driven task is the answer to this problem.

NCR, for example, has a large computer database that allows them to conduct in-house searches and evaluations, which are based on objective criteria. Using this database has routinely resulted in lists of candidates who might not otherwise have emerged. Another advantage of computerized searches is that information generated from the database encourages cross-divisional candidacies by making managers aware of qualified employees from other divisions.

Gerald L. McManis and Michael S. Leibman. Succession planners. *Personnel
    Administrator,* April 1988, pp. 24-30.

The authors discuss some lessons gleaned from succession plans at
organizations such as Exxon, Steelcase, and Sara Lee: (1) Top-management
support ensures that the succession plan has visibility and is taken seriously
by line management. (2) A succession plan should have clear principles and
objectives, which are tailored to the particular company. (3) Although the
succession system should be supported by the human resources department,
succession planning is a line-management tool. Even the best succession
plans will fail unless supported and driven by line management. At Exxon,
for example, line managers spend up to one-third of their time on succession
planning and human resources activities. (4) The succession plan must be
strongly linked to the business plan; as business changes demand different
skills and abilities, the succession plan must reflect these changes. (5) Keep
the succession plan as simple as possible; if the plan becomes too complex, it
is doomed to failure. Exxon, for example, operates its entire succession plan
through only four forms. (6) Because succession plans involve so much data,
automating the process through a variety of readily available software pack-
ages is highly recommended.

Richard Mirabile, David Caldwell, and Charles O'Reilly. Designing and
    linking human resource programs. *Training and Development Journal,*
    40:9, September 1986, pp. 60-65.

The authors argue that four human resources programs—selection and
assessment, career planning, management development, and succession
planning—have a common factor: Each deals in some way with skills and
abilities or competencies necessary for successful job performance. Thus,
they advocate a competency-based approach as a way to develop and integrate these four programs, and they provide a case study to show this can be
accomplished.
    The competency-based approach involves identifying the critical
managerial competencies for different levels of management. This information can then be used to enhance and link various human-resources programs.
It creates a valid method for assessment and selection by replacing generic
lists of competencies with lists of competencies specific to the organization
and for specific positions. Knowledge of these competencies benefits career-

planning, management-development, and succession-planning programs. This information can be used to assess the readiness levels of candidates for positions and to design developmental assignments that will help managers develop necessary competencies for upper-level positions; it also provides managers with awareness of the developmental activities they should embark on to prepare for various career paths.

❖ ❖ ❖

Kenneth W. Moore. Thoughts on management succession planning. *National Underwriter,* 90:45, 1986, p. 17.

Moore advises that when developing succession plans, the following guidelines should be kept in mind: Identify the positions that are to be included in the program, and describe the accountabilities of each position along with desired incumbent qualifications; for each position, create lists of candidates who are fully and partially qualified to assume the position; and develop logical and attainable career pathlines that will take employees up the corporate ladder.

Succession plans should be easy to operate and understand. Also, succession plans work best when tied with existing personnel systems within the organization, because employees are familiar with the system and generally trust it. Finally, organizational succession plans should be matched with individual development plans.

❖ ❖ ❖

National Academy of Public Administration. *Paths to leadership: Executive succession planning in the federal government.* Washington, DC: NAPA, December 1992, 125 pages.

This report presents the results of a comprehensive study on succession-planning practices in both the private and public sector. The study consisted of a literature review, encompassing more than 400 publications; colloquia with academic experts on succession planning; and forty on-site visits to private and public-sector organizations.

Seven characteristics of effective succession plans were identified: (1) Top-leadership involvement and commitment; (2) integration of strategic and succession planning; (3) compatibility with organizational culture; (4) attention to developing the careers of women and minorities and increasing the diversity of the executive ranks; (5) basing selections on well-developed competencies and assessments; (6) using job assignments as a primary executive-development tool, and making developmental assignments within the context of strategic plans; and (7) having the human resources group provide functional support for succession planning.

The literature review revealed several important lessons on succession planning: (1) Fight "groupthink" of senior executives. (2) Strategic thinking must focus on the organization's mission, not on individual positions. (3) Top management should make a significant time commitment (twenty-to-thirty percent of their time) to succession planning. (4) Succession-planning processes and procedures should be somewhat formalized, and responsibility for planning should be shared among executive trainers, succession-planners, and line executives; overly formalized systems, however, tend to emphasize form over substance. (5) Conduct periodic and objective human-resources reviews. (6) Rather than selecting high-potentials first and then developing them, organizations will be more successful if they develop first, then select. (7) Automated human-resources information systems have become an integral component of effective systems in succession planning.

✥ ✥ ✥

Gregory B. Northcraft, Terri L. Griffith, & Christiana E. Shalley. Building top management muscle in a slow growth environment: How different is better at Greyhound Financial Corporation. *Academy of Management Executive,* 6:1, 1992, pp. 32-40.

Greyhound Financial Corporation's "Muscle Building" program is a form of job rotation for top management; it focuses on both identifying and developing high-potentials. The number of new muscle-builders added to the program each year (two to four) is low, and positions are reserved for the highest-potential top executives at GFC. Once selected for the program, managers trade jobs and are placed in departments doing tasks different from those in their background and experience (for instance, the director of human resources management and the assistant vice president of real estate receivables switched jobs). The intent of the program is for high-potential managers to continue learning and developing, so once identified as a muscle-builder the manager will continue to receive new assignments every few years.

Because managers should be participating for development rather than monetary gain, they retain their basic compensation package and titles as they move through different developmental assignments. Most of the new assignments last for a couple of years to ensure that the manager has enough time to learn and excel in the new position. The program helps high-potentials gain broad experience and an organizational perspective and allows them to develop relationships with key players across the organization.

Gary R. Oddou and Mark E. Mendenhall. Succession planning for the 21st century: How well are we grooming our future business leaders? *Business Horizons,* 34:1, January-February 1991, pp. 26-34.

Surveys of 135 expatriate managers (representing primarily the electronics, aerospace, and banking industries) revealed that, overall, expatriation is a rich developmental opportunity. These managers reported experiencing a significant change in job responsibilities and more independence while overseas; they felt that these experiences significantly increased their global perspective of the firm's business operations, their ability to communicate effectively with people from diverse backgrounds, and their ability to conceptualize and comprehend business trends and events. However, they also reported that, upon repatriation, their firm failed to effectively reposition them or utilize their skills and international perspective.

The authors recommend that corporations "develop a strategic international human resource management system" (p. 67). This requires, first, thinking about what knowledge and skills will be required for a firm's future top management to make valid, globally strategic decisions in the future and, second, planning what types of positions and global experience will help prepare these individuals for future demands. High-potentials should receive overseas assignments as part of their development. In addition, technically proficient individuals from lower-level positions, who have not necessarily been identified as top-management potential but who will probably reach middle-management levels, should receive international assignments.

The authors also recommend: carefully preparing expatriates for their foreign assignments (for instance, providing survival language skills and cross-cultural communication skills); providing effective overseas support (for instance, expatriates need someone in the domestic operation responsible for maintaining contact with them as well as a mentor in the international operation); and furnishing effective reentry support and preparation (for instance, at least six months before the expatriate is to return, a position search should be initiated by the line manager in the domestic operation).

Patrick R. Pinto. *Succession planning: Paradigms, paradoxes, and "paradise."* Paper presented at the Annual Conference of the Human Resource Planning Society, Fort Lauderdale, FL, April 1992.

Pinto describes four primary approaches to succession planning: (1) Drop-dead charts: This is contingency planning which provides a ready replacement when a position suddenly becomes vacant; it tends to lack a developmental focus. (2) Crown prince and princess: Plans are made for a select few who are identified early as high-potentials. (3) Career development: Broad development and training programs that increase the skills of many employees are provided; the theme is often that career development begins with the individual. (4) Pools and flows: Planning involves identification of candidates for clusters of positions or levels and carefully managed mobility through the organization. Regardless of the approach, a "crisply defined purpose" is essential.

The author also identifies ten key paradoxes in succession planning and provides suggestions on how to deal with each:

(1) How do you promote from within but maintain a flow of outside talent? A healthy ratio of insiders to outsiders would be about eighty-five percent of positions that are filled; a higher percentage gets "dangerously close to inbreeding."

(2) How do you provide individuals with diverse experience when organizations today are leaner and flatter? Restructuring actually provides developmental opportunities, and leaner organizations mean that many jobs are richer in scope and complexity. In addition, it may prove useful to make people aware of the richness of experience available in their current jobs.

(3) How do you make your "hit rate" (percentage of positions actually filled annually by persons on the back-up list) not too high but just high enough? Strive to fill about two-thirds of positions with people from the back-up list.

(4) How do you provide individuals with honest feedback from assessments but maintain confidentiality? Be clear and open with individuals about their strengths and weaknesses, but take care not to identify who said what about them during the review process.

(5) How do you maintain corporate direction and consistency but support the unique needs of individual divisions? Develop a set of core competencies that serve as a common yardstick; this would provide consistency across divisions, while also meeting unique business situations.

(6) How do you fill positions with the best-fit candidate but provide stretch-learning assignments for individuals? This requires true commitment to development from top management.

(7) How do you focus on individual achievement, recognition, and mobility but tie the process to team-based management? Succession planning and team-based management are not necessarily incompatible, and even team-based total quality benefits from the development of individual skills. The team can also be used to assist individual development efforts (for instance, being assigned role of team leader).

(8) How do you simultaneously emphasize development of high-potential general managers as well as high-talent functional specialists? Separate the review process into multiple tracks; candidates for line positions are evaluated by line people, and professional managers and specialists are tracked through a functional review process.

(9) How do you prepare for the globalization of managers in a company that is currently domestic? Create strategic alliances with suppliers and vendors that are already in the marketplace.

(10) How do you encourage a positive human-resources functional role but keep the process line-driven? Emphasize mechanics, not the process. Managers must own the program and use human resources specialists as technical experts.

David W. Rhodes. Succession planning—overweight and underperforming. *The Journal of Business Strategy,* 9:6, November/December 1988, pp. 62-64.

Rhodes describes how succession planning as we know it today developed in the late 1960s and was designed to work in stable organizations. However, because of the rapid changes in organizations and the environment, succession plans of the 1990s are likely to fail. The problem is that most plans focus on too many objectives and too much data while failing to address the central challenge, which is to adapt "succession planning to help meet strategic staffing and development needs that will enable companies to keep pace with fundamental organizational and environmental changes" (p. 62). In fact, the author claims that succession planning is not worth the effort, because predicting succession over a long period of time in an era of constant change is becoming impossible.

An alternative to planning for succession is "developing talent": Instead of spending time anticipating vacancies and planning succession, organizations should focus on strategic staffing and development. "Succession planning as we know it today has run its course. In its place, we can expect to see a stronger focus on development of top-flight talent, the well-orchestrated movement of people, and the creation of executive education programs that keep managers working on real business problems" (p. 64). Rhodes concludes by suggesting ways that organizations can improve their succession plans (for instance, avoid developing succession and replacement charts and understand the characteristics that future managers will need to ensure the company's success).

David W. Rhodes and James W. Walker. Management succession and development planning. *Human Resource Planning,* 7:4, 1984, pp. 157-173.

The authors surveyed thirty large corporations about their management-succession practices and found that there is no single approach to succession planning but rather four different approaches: informal, decentralized, centralized, and integrated. The diversity among programs can be explained by four characteristics that differ among organizations: organization structure, management style, size and wealth, and company growth rate. For example, size and wealth will be related to resources made available for succession planning, and smaller, less complex companies will tend to have more informal succession plans. It is critical to consider these organizational characteristics before designing the succession-planning process. The authors advise that "the key to successful succession planning lies not in the development of sophisticated techniques, but in carefully matching the process to organizational characteristics" (p. 72).

These differences notwithstanding, there are recommendations for effective succession planning that apply to all companies. (1) Most important is the support and active involvement of the CEO and top management; without it, most corporate succession plans fail. (2) Although staff and senior-management support are critical, executive development should remain a line responsibility. (3) Managers should be held accountable for the development of their subordinates (for instance, specifically include development of subordinates as one aspect of the manager's performance evaluation). (4) Appraisal of succession candidates should be based on objective, job-related data, and evaluations should be made by more than one manager

familiar with the person's capabilities (that is, multirater assessment).
(5) Rather than keep succession plans a confidential process, which is typically the case, seek individual participation and input about career aspirations and developmental needs. (6) Rather than limit the identification of talent to a select few high-potentials, screening should be wide and flexible. (7) Movement of employees into developmental assignments should be carefully planned, and several techniques should be used. (8) Provide stretch assignments by placing candidates in assignments for which they are not fully qualified.

❖ ❖ ❖

William J. Rothwell. *Effective succession planning: Ensuring leadership continuity and building talent from within.* New York: AMACOM, 1994, 313 pages.

Rothwell provides basic guidelines on how to establish, operate, and evaluate succession-planning (SP) systems. The book is organized into four parts: part I (chapters 1 and 2)—an overview of SP; part II (chapters 3 to 5)—laying the foundation for an effective SP program; part III (chapters 6 and 7)—assessing work requirements in key positions and individual performance and potential; and part IV (chapters 8 to 10)—linking developmental strategies and SP. An epilogue addresses special issues in SP, such as incorporating diversity efforts and adapting to team environments. The book includes several activity guides and worksheets to assist SP efforts (for example, an interview guide for benchmarking practices in other companies, a worksheet to formulate a mission statement for the plan, a worksheet for preparing an action plan, sample outlines for in-house training, descriptions of various software programs, and a checklist for evaluating the SP program).

Chapters 1 and 2. Among human resources professionals, three of the most commonly cited reasons for having a formal SP program are: (1) to identify "replacement needs" as a means of targeting necessary training, employee education, and employee development; (2) to provide increased opportunities for high-potential workers; and (3) to increase the talent pool of promotable employees. Various approaches to SP can be categorized as traditional (involves developing people internally for key positions) and nontraditional (based on the premise that when a vacancy occurs, it does not necessarily need to be filled). Examples of nontraditional approaches include organization redesign (reallocate work duties to other key positions when a key position becomes vacant), process design (review a position first before automatically assuming that it needs to be replaced), and outsourcing (reassess whether activities of some key positions would be more cost-effectively handled externally). The important thing to remember is that there are numerous ways to ensure leadership continuity.

Chapter 2 includes a case study of Kmart to illustrate fifteen characteristics of effective SP programs. Common problems plaguing programs are also described. A "7-pointed star model" delineates steps for effective SP: "(1) Make the commitment to systematic SP, and establish an SP program. (2) Assess present work requirements. (3) Appraise individual performance. (4) Assess future work requirements. (5) Assess individual potential and use 360-degree feedback. (6) Close the developmental gap so as to meet SP needs. (7) Evaluate the SP program" (p. 59). These seven steps are the focus of chapters 3 to 10.

Chapters 3 and 4. Laying the foundation for an effective SP program requires the following steps. (1) Assess how current problems influence or are influenced by existing practices, and evaluate them. (2) Demonstrate the need for SP and obtain the support and time of key decision-makers by tying SP issues directly to the organization's pressing organizational problems and core mission. (3) Determine unique SP requirements, which depend on organizational differences such as industry, size, state of maturity, management values, and so on. Essential requirements should be linked to top-management's goals; identify these requirements by interviewing top managers. (4) Link the succession plan to organizational and human resources strategies. (5) Benchmark SP practices in other organizations to supplement information about unique organizational needs. (6) Obtain and build management commitment to systematic SP. Start-up of a program requires: clarifying the roles of individuals involved in the SP process; formulating a mission statement, which describes the purpose of the program; writing policies and procedures; identifying target groups for SP; and setting program priorities.

Chapter 5. Steps to be taken before an SP program can become operational are: (1) Prepare a program action plan, which outlines who should take what actions and when. This plan "activates and energizes an SP program" and provides a basis for accountability. (2) Communicate the action plan. (3) Conduct meetings. (4) Train key players on basics and objectives of effective SP.

Chapter 6. Identify "key positions" and work requirements of these positions through methods such as job- and task-analysis and competency assessment. Information on the performance of incumbents in key positions and prospective successors should be obtained via performance-appraisal data. Tailored SP software is becoming increasingly common as a method for keeping track of information on organizational work requirements and individual performance.

Chapter 7. Neither key positions nor their work requirements will remain static; strategies for determining future work requirements in key positions include conducting future-oriented job- and task-analysis and then assessing future competencies. Assessment of individual potential for performance in future positions, which should not be confused with present-oriented performance appraisal, can be accomplished through methods such as global assessment (asking senior executives for names of individuals whom they feel have high potential) or success-factor analysis (identifying traits, characteristics, and past experiences perceived to lead to organizational success or advancement; creating lists of success factors; and then rating subordinates against these factors). Approaches to individual potential assessment (IPA) range from the secretive "leader-driven" approach, in which employees have little say in the process, to "participative" or "empowered" individual assessment, in which the individual plays a central role in self-assessment and self-development; 360-degree feedback should be used for appraising the performance, potential, and developmental needs of succession candidates.

Chapter 8. Performance-appraisal data, IPA, and present and future work requirements should be used to determine how possible successors must be developed in preparation for future positions. Individual development plans (IDPs) outline activities designed to narrow the gap between what individuals can already do and what they should be able to do to meet future work requirements. Ten steps for developing an IDP are provided.

Chapter 9. Replacement for key positions is not always necessary (for example, if the position is no longer needed or if the position can be rendered unnecessary by reallocating duties to other positions within the organization). In such cases, strategists should explore alternatives to the traditional replacement-from-within approach to SP.

Chapter 10. A hierarchy of SP evaluation based on Kirkpatrick's *Hierarchy of Training Evaluation* is provided: level 1—customer satisfaction (How satisfied with the SP program and its components are its chief customers?); level 2—program progress (How well is the SP program working compared to stated objectives, and how well are individuals progressing through developmental plans?); level 3—effective placements (What percentage of vacancies in key positions has the organization filled internally, and how quickly and effectively have these positions been filled?); level 4—

organizational results (How is the SP program contributing to documentable organizational results?).

✜ ✜ ✜

Robert J. Sahl. Succession planning—a blueprint for your company's future. *Personnel Administrator,* 32:9, September 1987, pp. 101-106.

The closer the link between succession planning and other personnel systems, the more effective succession planning will be. The author describes five different levels of succession planning, which vary in their level of sophistication, with level 5 being the most sophisticated and at the optimal level.

Level 1 is the most informal level of succession planning, and it involves making a series of back-up charts. Decisions are often based on insufficient information and influenced by favoritism. Because of insufficient data, good candidates are often overlooked.

At level 2, performance-appraisal data are used as part of the identification process, which eliminates at least some subjectivity and favoritism—assuming that the performance-appraisal system is valid. At a minimum, companies should include levels 1 and 2 as part of the succession plan.

At level 3, in addition to performance-appraisal data, information is collected on individual career aspirations and potential. At this level, several personnel systems are interfacing: performance appraisal, succession planning, and career planning.

At level 4 the developmental needs of individuals are also considered, and plans are formulated to help prepare managers for future career positions. Thus, an additional personnel activity is added to the interface—management development.

At level 5, which incorporates all the components of levels 1 to 4, the size of promotions or developmental moves is also assessed (for instance, will a promotion be ten percent or twenty-five percent larger than the manager's current job?). This information can be obtained from the compensation program, thus linking succession planning to another personnel system.

✜ ✜ ✜

Jim Spoor. Succession planning: Once a luxury, now an emerging issue. *HR Focus*, December 1993, pp. 1, 4.

The author maintains that succession planning must be an integral part of strategic planning and that shared ownership of the process is critical; top line-and-staff management should all buy into the planning effort. The process should begin by identifying which positions will be included in the plan, keeping in mind how positions might change in the future and the impact of any changes reflected in the strategic plan. The position side of the plan should provide an estimate of what positions in the organization will look like in one, three, and five years. The next step involves identifying the competencies and skills required for each position.

On the candidate side of the process, efforts should focus on objective and accurate assessment of core competencies, along with consideration of individual career aspirations and preferences.

❖ ❖ ❖

Eric W. Vetter. Succession planning: Mastering the basics. *Human Resource Planning,* 7:2, 1984, pp. 99-104.

The author discusses why three established succession-planning assumptions are flawed and likely to meet with only limited success. First is the popular assumption that succession planning should be linked to business strategy. The business strategy is based on highly uncertain assumptions; therefore, specific details of the strategic plan should not be of concern but rather the general strategic issue of how to recruit and develop the types of managers the organization will need in the future.

A second assumption is that, in order to improve the quality of succession-planning decisions, information should be integrated through a sophisticated computer system. Yet, in reality, decision-makers often want qualitative, firsthand data, not sterile computer printouts.

The third assumption is that organizational movement should be used for management development. However, because of economic pressures and downsizing, organizations have eliminated many developmental positions, and there are few rewards for the manager who develops his or her subordinates.

The author advocates that in place of these techniques, organizations should focus on mastering the basics of succession planning: (1) Perfect the art of "doing the doable" rather than seeking the newest techniques; the process should focus on establishing realistic objectives and aim for a seventy-five percent success rate. (2) Design an information system that provides all of the relevant information in an easy-to-use form, and avoid information overload. (3) Allocate sufficient time for review sessions; discussion during these sessions should be open, thorough, and provocative. (4) Each review session should result in specific outcomes that must be completed during the next twelve months by an accountable manager. Proposed actions should be put in written form and updated quarterly for progress information; this ensures that succession planning is taken seriously and that planned actions don't fall by the wayside as more immediate pressing business concerns emerge.

James W. Walker. *Human resource planning*. New York: McGraw-Hill, 1980, pp. 274-306.

In a chapter entitled "Management succession and development planning," Walker says that commitment to the development of employees and the intentional movement of individuals to assignments for developmental purposes, even when not in the best interest of short-term business necessity, is a critical part of succession planning. Furthermore, the assessment of managerial potential must focus on objective criteria rather than subjective factors; succession plans must remain a line responsibility; and developmental/succession plans should be based on an organizational needs analysis.

More specifically, succession planning should include the following components: (1) biographical data on prospective candidates, including career progress, experience, career interests and aspirations, and so forth; (2) evaluation of individual performance against established goals or standards and feedback of results; (3) determination of future management-staffing requirements; (4) creation of "position profiles" that define requirements of future managerial positions; (5) managerial review, which involves discussion of these data—the heart of the process; (6) a tailored development plan for each succession candidate, which provides plans for bridging the gaps in individual capabilities relative to targeted position requirements; (7) summaries of candidate availability and readiness to step into various management assignments. More specific guidelines for succession planning are covered and include the functions of a review committee, defining managerial and future position requirements, and designing management-development activities.

Obstacles to management development include: (1) fragmentation, where departments or divisions operate independently and look after their own talent; (2) informality, where managers rely on their own personal knowledge of candidates (individual-development potential and needs being based on subjective assessments rather than objective job standards and requirements); (3) an emphasis on short-term planning perspectives and short-term business concerns, which impedes implementation of long-term development plans; (4) overlooking individual aspirations, goals, and preferences and manipulating careers in the interest of short-term business needs rather than individual development.

❖ ❖ ❖

Peter Wallum. A broader view of succession planning. *Personnel Management,* 25:9, September 1993, pp. 42-45.

A survey of senior executives from nineteen major international companies revealed that, although career planning and succession planning have traditionally been two separate systems, leading organizations are beginning to fuse the two. The advantage of this fusion is that it guarantees a suitable supply of successors for key and future jobs, while also meeting individual career needs and aspirations.

Because most organizations are continually changing and reallocating executive responsibilities, the focus of succession planning should not only be on competencies for current jobs. Successful plans must also focus on defining managerial competencies to meet future roles arising from business strategy. Respondents reported that succession planning was more successful when driven by line management.

❖ ❖ ❖

Section 2: Commonly Reported Succession-planning Practices in Organizations—Descriptions from the Literature

The authors of the fifty-six annotated references above are from different disciplines and orientations—for instance, organizational researchers, human resources managers, and consultants. Despite the diversity of their backgrounds and approaches, they have nonetheless expressed some common views about effective succession-planning systems.

1. The Succession Plan Receives Visible Support from the CEO and Top Management.

Visible support and commitment of the CEO and top management are cited as cardinal elements of succession planning. In fact, some experts have suggested that without support and involvement from the top of the organization, even the best succession plans are doomed for failure (Clark & Lyness, 1991; Executive Knowledgeworks, 1988; Friedman, 1986; Hall, 1984; Hall & Foulkes, 1990; Lee, 1981). Rothwell (1994) warns that "if top managers are unwilling to support a systematic approach to succession planning, it cannot succeed" (p. 49).

Based on their experience with succession plans in a variety of organizations, Mahler and Drotter (1986) concluded that a major requirement of succession planning is top-management action: Top management must make a commitment to and actively participate in the succession-planning process. Similarly, the National Academy of Public Administration (1992) recently conducted a comprehensive study of succession-planning practices in both the private and public sector and concluded that top-leadership involvement and commitment is a common characteristic of successful succession plans.

Visible support and commitment from the CEO and top management ensure that the succession plan has visibility and is taken seriously by line management (McManis & Leibman, 1988). According to Buckner and Slavenski (1994), top-management support gives succession planning a sense of urgency and importance in getting things done and, therefore, is probably the most important factor in instigating a successful program. Organizations, too, commonly report that extensive and visible involvement by the CEO and top management is the single greatest determinant of a program's success or failure (Borwick, 1991 [part 1]; Carnazza, 1982; Fenwick-Magrath, 1988; Leibman & Bruer, 1994).

2. The Succession Plan Is Owned by Line Management and Supported by Staff.

Shared ownership of the succession plan is reported to be critical; both line management and staff should be actively involved in the process, and their responsibilities should be clearly defined (Kramer, 1990; National Academy of Public Administration, 1992; Spoor, 1993). Line management should assume ownership of the process and responsibility for identifying and developing talent for succession, while staff should facilitate the process by providing technical expertise, functional support, and access to helpful succession-planning tools (Borwick, 1991 [part 2]; Buckner & Slavenski, 1994; Cowherd, 1986; Hernandez, Haddock, Behrendt, & Klein, 1991; Kramer, 1990). As asserted by Pinto (1992), line managers must own the process and use human resources specialists as technical experts.

Several writers suggest that staff should provide support yet avoid taking complete ownership of the succession-planning process or creating the perception that it owns the process (Borwick, 1991 [part 2]; Fenwick-Magrath, 1988; Pinto, 1992). "The staff's role is to serve as an internal consultant, advising line management and providing whatever programs or services they need, but not to serve as the driving force behind the effort" (Executive Knowledgeworks, 1988, p. 52). Staff should act as a "catalyst" and actively interact, stimulate, and push the process along, while still keeping neutral in the process (Mahler & Drotter, 1986).

This imperative is supported by findings from a survey of Fortune 500 firms: Friedman (1986) examined the relationship between staff role—the extent to which human resources professionals were involved in and took ownership of succession planning—and corporate reputation and financial performance. He found that staff credibility and access to needed information were positively related to organizational performance but that staff ownership of the succession-planning process, that is, less line ownership, was associated with lower performance. Thus, Friedman concluded that staff should be actively involved with succession planning but that the responsibility ultimately remains with line management.

Borwick (1993) proposes that the majority of succession-planning decisions should be made by line management because: (a) The more management layers involved in succession planning, the less effective communication and feedback will be, and (b) line management is closest to the business context. Other succession-planning experts concur that the effectiveness of a succession plan relies most heavily upon the commitment, support, and active participation of line management. Companies also report that succession planning is most successful when driven by line management (Executive Knowledgeworks, 1988; Fenwick-Magrath, 1988; Friedman, 1986; Kramer, 1990; Mahler & Drotter, 1986; McManis & Leibman, 1988; Rhodes & Walker, 1984; Wallum, 1993).

In reality, however, succession planning frequently becomes the responsibility of human resources while line management ignores the process—a common explanation for the limited effectiveness of succession planning (Borwick, 1991 [part 1]; Executive Knowledgeworks, 1988). As Leibman and Bruer (1994) noted, too often succession planning is a once-a-year paper process during which line managers are surveyed and huge notebooks are compiled by the human resources department. Kramer (1990) discusses how to design a system that encourages line ownership, for example, by conducting a thorough needs analysis to ensure that the succession plan is designed to meet the requirements of line management. At Corning, line ownership is encouraged by continuous feedback: Human resources managers talk with each line manager several times during the year regarding succession-planning concerns (Leibman & Bruer, 1994).

3. The Succession Plan Is Simple and Tailored to Unique Organizational Needs.

The succession plan should be kept as simple as possible and easy to operate (Mahler & Drotter, 1986; McManis & Leibman, 1988; Moore, 1986; Spoor, 1993). Although succession-planning processes and procedures should be somewhat formalized, overly formalized systems tend to emphasize form over substance and do not necessarily improve chances of success (National Academy of Public Administration, 1992). Friedman (1986) found that the extent to which written rules and procedures existed for succession planning was not related to organizational performance, thus indicating that "formalization may be a necessary but not sufficient condition for effective succession systems" (p. 95).

The succession-planning system should have a mission statement which describes the purpose of the system, who it will serve, and the desired outcomes. These statements will vary across organizations, and Rothwell (1994) provides a list of issues that should be addressed by the mission statement (pp. 103-104). In addition, the succession plan must be tailored to the organization's culture, characteristics, and operating environment (Beatty, Schneier, & McEvoy, 1987; Fenwick-Magrath, 1988; Gratton & Syrett, 1990; Hansen & Wexler, 1988; Mahler, 1981; Mahler & Drotter, 1986; McManis & Leibman, 1988; National Academy of Public Administration, 1992).

Succession-planning requirements will not be the same across organizations, and organizational characteristics, such as structure, size, wealth, growth rate, maturity, and management values are all factors that must be taken into account when designing a plan (Carnazza, 1982; Executive Knowledgeworks, 1988; National Academy of Public Administration, 1992; Rhodes & Walker, 1984; Rothwell, 1994). For example, size and wealth will be related to resources available for succession planning, and smaller, less complex companies will tend to have less formal succession plans (Rhodes & Walker, 1984); and the succession-planning needs will be different for a company that is in a rapid-growth mode versus one that is characterized by slow growth or decline.

Buckner and Slavenski (1994) suggest that the succession plan can only be designed after "profiling the organization" and evaluating a number of issues. For example: Are business units centrally managed or decentralized? What are the positions needing successors? And what problem is the organization trying to solve? Rothwell (1994) recommends beginning the succession-planning process by interviewing top management to determine what they believe are the succession plan's essential requirements. In addition to ensuring that the plan meets the organization's unique needs, this approach is also more likely to secure the support and commitment of top management.

Although the literature reviewed here suggests that there are core elements common to effective succession-planning systems, these works demonstrate that plans vary considerably across companies and there is no "best" plan. The most effective plans are tailored to specific organizational needs, and simply borrowing succession plans from other successful companies is unlikely to meet a company's unique needs (Carnazza, 1982; Fenwick-Magrath, 1988; Mahler, 1981; Mahler & Drotter, 1986; Rhodes & Walker, 1984). The succession plan should not be "a template program or a prefabricated format imposed upon an organization [but rather] defined from within the company and highly company specific" (Borwick, 1991 [part 2], p. 2). Gratton and Syrett (1990) describe four different, but equally effective, approaches to succession planning to demonstrate that there is no universal approach to succession planning, and Hernandez, Haddock, Behrendt, and Klein (1991) explain how a succession plan was developed to meet the specific needs of an organization.

Though tailoring the succession plan to meet the organization's unique needs is essential, information from other organizations with effective succession plans can be used to guide or augment a company's succession-planning process: Rothwell (1994) advocated establishing a needs-driven program with external benchmarks; the succession plan should be tailored to specific organizational needs while simultaneously taking advantage of the state-of-the-art approaches from organizations with a history of success with succession planning. For example, Kmart's succession-planning program began by identifying specific business needs that the plan would need to address; at the same time, the succession-planning coordinator made benchmarking visits to organizations with reputations for effective succession-planning practices (Rothwell, 1994).

4. The Succession Plan Is Flexible and Linked with Strategic Business Plan.

The succession plan should be an evolving and iterative process that reflects any significant changes in the strategic plan (Mahler & Gaines, 1983). According to Borwick (1991 [part 2]), the traditional approach to succession planning was established in the 1950s and is based on the premise that individuals should be matched with statically defined positions; this approach, however, is outdated and conflicts with the rapidly changing needs of today's organizations.

Instead, succession planning should be "an ongoing process like the business planning itself" (Leibman & Bruer, 1994, p. 28). Rapid organizational and environmental changes call for a flexible succession plan which is intricately linked to the strategic business plan and designed to respond to evolving organizational needs (Borwick, 1991 [part 2], 1993; Buckner & Slavenski, 1994; Carnazza, 1982; Clark & Lyness, 1991; Fenwick-Magrath, 1988; Friedman, 1986; Hall & Seibert, 1991; Kesner, 1989; Lee, 1981; Mahler, 1981; National Academy of Public Administration, 1992; Rhodes, 1988; Rothwell, 1994; Walker, 1980).

Moreover, both the demands of key positions and the skills and abilities required of people in these positions will fluctuate with changes going on in the business, and the succession plan must reflect such changes (Allison, 1993; McManis & Leibman, 1988; Rothwell, 1994). Organizations should first review their business plans before discussing individuals and positions; then they should ask more specific questions such as, "What types of people will we need in the future to achieve our strategies and goals?" (Kramer, 1990). Borwick (1991 [part 1]) maintains that, although most plans are isolated from the company's business goals, ideally the organization should view business results as the ultimate end and the succession plan as the means to that end.

Involving the same executives in both the management-development reviews and the strategic business-planning meetings helps strengthen the link between the succession plan and business strategy (Clark & Lyness, 1991; Leibman & Bruer, 1994). Implementing the succession plan in phases and continuously reviewing the process so that it is tailored to specific business needs is another way to establish the essential link between business strategy and the succession plan (Borwick, 1991 [part 2], 1992 [part 3]; Kramer, 1990; Rothwell, 1994). Continuously reviewing progress ensures that the plan reflects important organizational priorities and changes while also maintaining the plan's vitality (Getty, 1993). Borwick (1993) also advises that, rather than viewing succession planning as an end in itself, the focus should be on continuously improving the process, and Hansen and Wexler (1988) argue that "one sure measure of an ineffective system is that it does not change over time" (p. 100).

Despite the touted benefits of linking the strategic business plan and succession plan, this practice is not very common (Executive Knowledgeworks, 1988). Succession plans in most organizations focus on replacing positions as they exist today and are divorced from any long-term plan or business strategy (Allison, 1993; Hall, 1986; Hall & Foulkes, 1990; Hall & Seibert, 1991). It has been suggested that this schism between succession planning and business strategy is one of the primary reasons that succession plans fail (Borwick, 1991 [part 1]; Carnazza, 1982; Hall, 1984, 1986; Hall & Foulkes, 1990).

5. The Succession Plan Evolves from a Thorough Human-resources Review Process.

According to the literature reviewed here, periodic human-resources review meetings typically provide the forum for identifying succession candidates and planning for their development. Some organizations conduct several of these reviews at the department, division, and corporate levels, and other organizations may conduct only one review, in which a few of the very senior executives participate (Executive Knowledgeworks, 1988). Several authors on the subject have suggested that the review process should not be restricted to top levels of management; it should be a bottom-up process, wherein the process begins in the division and functional areas and is based on input from a large group of managers. Top-level management then reviews the recommendations and makes revisions (Borwick, 1993; Buckner & Slavenski, 1994; Fenwick-Magrath, 1988; Getty, 1993; Mahler & Gaines, 1983).

Mahler and Drotter (1986) contend that the review meeting is the most important aspect of a succession-planning system. Buckner and Slavenski (1994) claim that the review meeting is essential because it creates the energy for completing the succession-planning process, it gives top management the opportunity to provide support, and job moves and developmental actions are more likely to occur when managers openly discuss candidates. Rothwell (1994) also claims that periodic review meetings are crucial for the success of a succession-planning program, because it helps keep the program on target and emphasizes the importance of succession planning to key executives.

Key players should be present at the review meeting, and the quality of preparation for this meeting should be high: Executives should come prepared to engage in thorough and open discussions regarding key issues such as the linkage between succession planning and strategic business plans, the identification and discussion of succession candidates, developmental plans for succession candidates, and special programs, such as affirmative action (Borwick, 1993; Buckner & Slavenski, 1994; Getty, 1993; Mahler & Drotter, 1986; Mahler & Gaines, 1983; National Academy of Public Administration, 1992; Rothwell, 1994; Vetter, 1984; Walker, 1980).

To improve the quality of the review process in organizations with separate functions or business units, Getty (1993) suggests broadening views: Succession plans should be presented in a group format in which top managers present their succession plan for their individual units; this approach prevents organizations from developing a narrow view of where talent can be found and helps managers learn about talent outside of their area. Mahler (1981) found that tutoring executives in how to prepare for the review process is one way to improve the quality of discussions and plans made during the review meeting. Kramer (1990) recommends asking managers to complete a questionnaire at the end of the review session to find out what they liked and did not like about the process and what changes should be made to the system.

6. The Succession Plan Is Based Upon Well-developed Competencies and Objective Assessment of Candidates.

The literature reviewed here suggests that succession planning involves clearly defining the requirements and requisite competencies for key positions and then identifying which employees should be developed to fill these positions in the future. To ensure that this is a fair and effective process, decisions should be based on systematic analyses of: (1) job requirements (both current and projected) of upper-level positions; and (2) the current performance levels and potential of individual employees (Rothwell, 1994). Effective succession-planning systems are based on well-defined competencies and reliable information about the current performance and potential of employees (National Academy of Public Administration, 1992).

To begin, key positions should be identified, and the requirements for these positions should be defined; job analysis can be used to identify competencies for key positions in highly technical and stable organizations; in flexible organizations, more general competencies should be established (Buckner & Slavenski, 1994; Executive Knowledgeworks, 1988; Kramer, 1990).

Burnett and Waters (1984) recommend using the action profile to identify requirements of upper-level positions. The action profile is "a description, in behavioral terms, of the managerial capacities, skills, and personal qualities required in a particular position" (p. 16). The advantage of this profile is that it describes upper-level management positions in objective job-related terms, while also providing a common metric for assessing potential and readiness of succession candidates for particular positions.

Competency assessments for key positions can also be obtained using a variety of methods, for example, merging a list of "generic management leadership competencies" along with "organization-specific competencies" to create an "executive success profile" (Rothwell, 1994).

In-depth interviews with representatives from sixty-four U.S. corporations revealed that effective succession plans are based on two types of information: (1) information about general managerial requirements for the organization overall, and (2) information about specific job criteria for specific positions covered by the plan (Executive Knowledgeworks, 1988). That is, the competencies for upper-level management positions should be defined at the general strategic level (for example, What kind of managers will we need in the future?) and at the specific job level.

Because most organizations are continuously changing, the focus of succession planning should not only be on competencies for current jobs; successful plans must also focus on determining how jobs and organizational roles might change in the future and then define competencies needed to meet these changes (Rothwell, 1994; Wallum, 1993). Spoor (1993) recommends developing competency profiles based on an estimate of what positions in the organizations will look like in one, three, and five years. Rothwell (1994) also discusses methods for projecting requirements of future key positions, such as conducting future-oriented job analysis and determining the associated competencies required for success.

The identification of succession candidates should be based upon objective, job-related assessments and ratings of promotability or readiness for future positions (Beatty et al., 1987; Friedman, 1986; Kramer, 1990; Lee, 1981; Mahler & Drotter, 1986; McElwain, 1991; National Academy of Public Administration, 1992; Rhodes & Walker, 1984). But in many organizations, subjective and anecdotal assessments of candidates prevail in the succession-planning process; as a result, management often fails to identify all the best candidates, and those considered for advancement or developmental placements are simply those who have become most visible to senior management; furthermore, when relying on subjective assessments, top executives tend to choose successors similar to themselves rather than identify managers with skills and experiences needed to succeed in the future (Borwick, 1991 [part 1]; Cowherd, 1986; Hall, 1986; Hall & Foulkes, 1990; Mahler & Drotter, 1986; National Academy of Public Administration, 1992; Rothwell, 1994; Walker, 1980).

To limit the role of subjective assessments and anecdotal assessments, succession candidates should be identified through formal assessment methods such as performance appraisal and other sources of job-relevant information, such as psychological tests and assessment centers (Beatty et al., 1987; Buckner & Slavenski, 1994). Objective and job-relevant assessment data help effectively identify succession candidates, while also providing essential information regarding the developmental needs of these candidates (Executive Knowledgeworks, 1988; Hinrichs & Hollenbeck, 1990; Rhodes & Walker, 1984).

Performance-appraisal data, which help identify which employees are exemplary performers, are an important source of information for succession planning (Mahler & Gaines, 1983; Rothwell, 1994). A survey of representatives from sixty-four U.S. corporations revealed that a majority of companies (95%) with successful plans reported formal evaluation of candidates, a process that usually was tied to the performance-appraisal system (Executive Knowledgeworks, 1988).

General Electric's accomplishment analysis, which stresses past accomplishments as an indicator of future performance, is another example of information that can be used to evaluate potential successors: An executive consultant interviews a succession candidate for three-to-four hours and may also interview former associates and subordinates; a written summary of the individual's achievements and possible developmental plans is the outcome of this assessment (Friedman & LeVino, 1984; Mahler, 1981).

In addition to assessing past performance, employees should also be evaluated for their potential for success in future upper-level positions: Multi-rater instruments, which provide feedback from a variety of sources, such as subordinates, bosses, and peers (that is, 360-degree feedback), are useful for assessing both an individual's current performance and potential for future positions, and therefore, are valuable sources of information for succession planning (Rothwell, 1994). For example, at Royal Bank of Canada, a 360-degree evaluation of managers is used to identify high-potentials for succession planning, and Kmart uses 360-degree assessment results to identify high-potentials and the developmental needs of those individuals (Drake, 1993; Rothwell, 1994).

According to Buckner and Slavenski (1994), one of the best formal methods for assessing employee promotability or potential is the use of assessment centers, because they have a high degree of predictability of success at more senior levels. Beatty, Schneier, and McEvoy (1987) advise that, when assessing the match between candidates and future positions, it is not enough to consider the nature of competencies and traits required for successful performance in upper-level positions. An additional issue is the organizational context: The organization's culture, life-cycle stage, technology, degree of risk associated with decision making, and the type of feedback cycle should all be considered. The assessment of executive/organization match should involve comparing each potential executive's skills-and-competencies profile with the organization's requirements in terms of tasks, roles, culture, risk, feedback, and technology.

Borwick (1991 [part 2], 1992 [part 3]) recommends that, given the growing importance of teams in organizations, succession planning should involve collecting data on teams as well as individual positions and individual candidates. Similarly, Leibman and Bruer (1994) claim that "instead of identifying the right person for the right position at the right time, corporations are looking to continually develop strong leadership *teams* for strategic *tasks*" (p. 29).

Several experts advocate PC (personal computer) automation for effectively managing the vast amounts of data generated by succession planning (Butterill, 1990; McElwain, 1991; McManis & Leibman, 1988; National Academy of Public Administration, 1992; Spoor, 1993), and tailored succession-planning software is becoming more common (Rothwell, 1994). Especially in larger organizations, PC automation helps simplify data collection and integrate the succession-planning system with other personnel systems (Buckner & Slavenski, 1994; Rothwell, 1994).

Brush and Nardoni (1992) discuss the advantages of their microcomputer-based succession-planning system at AT&T and outline general requirements for organizations considering a computerized succession-planning system (for example, the system should have extensive data capacity and the ability to link the succession plan to other management staffing and career-development systems). Others contend that succession planning is not contingent on the prowess of a sophisticated computer system, but rather on the quality and relevance of the information collected (Borwick, 1993; Buckner & Slavenski, 1994; Vetter, 1984).

7. The Succession Plan Incorporates Employee Input.

The literature reviewed here suggests that, in addition to information on the requirements of upper-level management positions and objective assessment data on potential successors, the succession plan should incorporate information on the career needs and aspirations of individual employees. Succession planning should be a collaborative process designed to meet the career needs of the individual as well as the organization (Mahler, 1981).

Buckner and Slavenski (1994) contend that the best succession-planning system is one that meets the needs of both the organization and its employees. Accordingly, the process of succession planning should involve collecting data from employees about their career aspirations, career interests, willingness to relocate or assume new positions, developmental needs, and assignments that they think would most contribute to their long-term development (Allison, 1993; Borwick, 1992 [part 3]; Clark & Lyness, 1991; Getty, 1993; Gratton & Syrett, 1990; Hall, 1986; Lee, 1981; Mahler, 1981; Mahler & Drotter, 1986; Rhodes & Walker, 1984; Spoor, 1993; Walker, 1980).

However, the literature points out that the clandestine nature of succession planning in many organizations often precludes employee involvement, and succession plans emphasize organizational needs without regard to the needs and interests of individual employees. When formulating succession plans, decision-makers rarely consider a candidate's willingness or desire to assume a new position, relocate, or to engage in developmental activities (Borwick, 1993; Buckner & Slavenski, 1994; Carnazza, 1982; Getty, 1993; Hall, 1986). The danger of this approach is that employees may refuse promotions or new positions that conflict with their career goals and needs (Rothwell, 1994).

Employee input can be obtained by asking employees to complete career-interest forms that assess issues such as willingness to relocate, career goals, and work preferences (Buckner & Slavenski, 1994). Moreover, in preparation for the human resources review process, supervisors can conduct developmental reviews and career discussions—which are not linked to compensation—with their subordinates (Friedman & LeVino, 1984; Hernandez et al., 1991; Rothwell, 1994).

Using assessment results, such as performance appraisal and 360-degree feedback, employees can work together with their supervisor to create an individual development plan that is tailored to their particular developmental needs and career goals (Hernandez et al., 1991; McCauley, Eastman, & Ohlott, 1995). At Pepsi-Cola Corporation, for example, employees go through a performance-appraisal/developmental feedback process with their supervisors. From this, a profile of the person's developmental needs, strengths, and career plans is constructed (Drake, 1993).

The advantage of incorporating employee input into the planning process is twofold: (a) It encourages individual managers to accept responsibility for their own development, and (b) it more effectively meets the needs of both the organization and individual succession-candidates (Buckner & Slavenski, 1994; Friedman & LeVino, 1984; Hernandez et al., 1991; Rothwell, 1994).

8. The Succession Plan Is Part of Broader Management-development Effort.

Planning how to develop employees for upper-level positions and future organizational demands is a central feature of effective succession-planning systems (Carnazza, 1982; National Academy of Public Administration, 1992; Rothwell, 1994). Management development should be intricately linked with the succession plan, and it should receive top priority (Hall, 1984, 1986; Hansen & Wexler, 1988; Hernandez et al., 1991; Walker, 1980). Hall and Foulkes (1990) argue that succession planning should be linked to both the future direction of the organization and the learning and development of managers. Similarly, Hall and Siebert (1991) have proposed what they refer to as *strategic management development*—focusing on anticipated future management positions and the expected skills requirements of these positions, and developing people for these positions—as a way to link organizational strategy, succession planning, and managerial learning.

Once the requirements of upper-level positions and succession candidates have been identified, decision-makers must plan how they will provide developmental opportunities that will prepare candidates for future organizational demands (Beatty et al., 1987; Executive Knowledgeworks, 1988; Hansen & Wexler, 1988; Moore, 1986). For each succession candidate there should be an individual development plan (IDP), which outlines planned activities that will help "narrow the gap between what individuals can already do and what they should do to meet future work requirements of one or more positions" (Rothwell, 1994, p. 218). IDPs should be tailored to the unique needs of each candidate and should focus on three major categories: work experiences and assignments, coaching, and educational courses and seminars (Kramer, 1990; Mahler & Gaines, 1983; Walker, 1980). Rothwell (1994) outlines ten steps to follow when developing an IDP.

A pitfall of many succession-planning systems is that they emphasize the identification and assessment of talent, while paying less attention to development (Cowherd, 1986; Hall, 1986; Hall & Foulkes, 1990; Hall & Seibert, 1991; Mahler & Drotter, 1986). Nonetheless, concern about bench strength and the fact that fewer employees are making lifelong careers in one organization have led some experts to suggest that development of talent will become more crucial than the actual replacement-planning aspect of succession planning. For example, Rhodes (1988) advocates developing talent: Instead of spending time anticipating vacancies and planning succession, organizations should focus on strategic staffing and development. Hall (1986) has proposed that organizations will experience more success with succession planning if they develop first and then select. Similarly, the National Academy of Public Administration's (1992) extensive review of the succession-planning literature and practices led to the conclusion that, rather than select high-potentials first and then develop them, organizations will be more successful if they develop first, then select.

Succession planning can prepare women and minorities for upper-level management positions by ensuring that they receive substantial developmental opportunities (Borwick, 1992 [part 3]; Hernandez et al., 1991; National Academy of Public Administration, 1992). Monitoring the developmental tracks of these employees seems especially important in light of a study of Fortune 500 firms, which revealed that succession-planning programs were most successful in promoting white males and less successful in advancing women and minorities (Curtis & Russell, 1993).

It is important to note that individual employees and the organization must *both* assume responsibility for development: The organization should provide ample developmental opportunities along with the necessary support for development, such as developmental feedback and access to coaches or mentors (McCall, 1992; McCauley et al., 1995; Rothwell, 1994); but the organization must also convey the message that the ultimate responsibility for development lies with the individual first and the organization second

(Hansen & Wexler, 1988; Hernandez et al., 1991; Hinrichs & Hollenbeck, 1990). Encouraging employees to take personal responsibility for development is critical given the prediction that managers of the future increasingly will need to be self-learners in order to adapt to rapid organizational changes (Baldwin & Padgett, 1993; Hall & Foulkes, 1990; Hall & Seibert, 1991).

9. The Succession Plan Includes Plans for Developmental Job Assignments.

The frequent opportunity for employees to accept new job challenges is a characteristic of effective succession-planning systems (McElwain, 1991; Rothwell, 1994). Although executive-development practices traditionally have relied on formal educational programs, there is a growing awareness that managers learn primarily from challenging job experiences, such as task forces, job rotations, line-to-staff switches, and turnaround or fix-it assignments (Baldwin & Padgett, 1993; Buckner & Slavenski, 1994; Derr, Jones, & Toomey, 1988; Fenwick-Magrath, 1988; Hinrichs & Hollenbeck, 1990; Mahler & Drotter, 1986; McCauley et al., 1995). Job rotations or "broadening moves," in which high-potentials are given assignments that expose them to critical aspects of the business, are a common form of executive development that help prepare individuals for more senior-level positions in the organization (Beatty et al., 1987; Derr et al., 1988; Rothwell, 1994).

Downsizing and delayering have eliminated several promotional opportunities traditionally earmarked for high-potentials; consequently, companies increasingly will need to make an effort to create developmental assignments, such as lateral moves and job rotations, for their succession candidates (Friedman, 1990; Hall, 1989; Hall & Foulkes, 1990; Hinrichs & Hollenbeck, 1990). At Weyerhaeuser, for example, succession planning involves meshing developmental opportunities with upcoming business challenges, and "real live experiences" are used to provide the "grist" for executive development (Leibman & Bruer, 1994). Kmart uses developmental experiences to familiarize high-potentials with the corporate environment and culture and to help foster knowledge and skills that are essential for higher organizational levels in the company.

Developmental assignments should be long enough to allow sufficient time for learning to occur (approximately two-to-three years), because too-rapid movement results in insufficient time to benefit from the developmental opportunities in a given assignment (Buckner & Slavenski, 1994; Derr et al., 1988; Executive Knowledgeworks, 1988; Mahler & Drotter, 1986). It is important to have line managers involved in planning these moves and to get

their support for moving people between organizational areas (Buckner &
Slavenski, 1994; Kramer, 1990).

    Similar to other aspects of succession planning, developmental assign-
ments should be made within the context of the strategic plan (Baldwin &
Padgett, 1993; Hall, 1984; National Academy of Public Administration,
1992). For example, the growing importance of international experience
indicates that overseas assignments will become a prevalent developmental
strategy for future top-level and middle-level managers (Oddou &
Mendenhall, 1991).

    Succession planning requires intentional movement of individuals
among assignments for developmental purposes, even when not in the best
interest of short-term business necessity (Hinrichs & Hollenbeck, 1990;
Walker, 1980). Placing candidates in assignments for which they are not fully
qualified—stretch assignments—creates a rich developmental opportunity;
the novelty and challenges of a new job situation stretch the person beyond
his or her current abilities (Friedman, 1986; Hinrichs & Hollenbeck, 1990;
McCall, 1992; McCauley et al., 1995; McElwain, 1991; Rhodes & Walker,
1984). Citicorp, for instance, tries to place high-potentials into jobs for which
they are no more than sixty-to-seventy percent qualified (Clark & Lyness,
1991). (See McCauley, Eastman, and Ohlott [1995] for a more in-depth
discussion of how to incorporate stretch assignments with succession planning. Also, see Northcraft, Griffith, and Shalley [1992] for an example of
how stretch assignments are used to groom future talent.)

10. The Succession Plan Is Integrated with Other Human-resources Systems.

    The succession plan should not function as an isolated system but rather
as an integral component of the overall human-resources planning process
(Beatty et al., 1987). Organizations should review other human-resources
procedures and policies to determine how the plan will work in relation to
these programs (Kramer, 1990). Rothwell (1994) contends that succession
planning will be most effective when human resources practices are reviewed
and designed to facilitate rather than impede succession-planning efforts. Sahl
(1987) and Mahler and Drotter (1986) also assert that the closer the link
between the succession plan and other personnel systems, the more effective
planning efforts will be.

    As implied by the key practices stated above, the most effective succes-
sion plans are closely integrated with and build upon available information
from existing human-resources systems, such as performance appraisal,

management development, training and development, compensation, EEO and affirmative action, career planning, and recruitment (Borwick, 1992 [part 3]; Buckner & Slavenski, 1994; Executive Knowledgeworks, 1988; Hernandez et al., 1991; Moore, 1986). For example, corporations commonly report using performance-appraisal data for the assessment and identification of succession candidates, and management-development efforts help prepare these candidates for future upper-level positions. Combining succession- and career-planning systems is also crucial (Butterill, 1990; Hall, 1986), and leading organizations are beginning to fuse these traditionally separate entities (Wallum, 1993). As Leibman and Bruer (1994) conclude, "Radical changes can be accomplished if succession planning is viewed not simply as a series of isolated events, but is inculcated with the ongoing management of the business and development of executive resources" (p. 29).

Burdett (1993) explains how a job-competencies approach (identifying in behavioral terms the essential characteristics for job success) has helped link performance appraisal, career planning, and succession planning at Lawson Mardon Group. This approach provides objective and job-relevant data for assessment purposes and developmental planning, while also linking the succession plan to other critical personnel systems. Similarly, Mirabile, Caldwell, and O'Reilly (1986) advocate a job-competency approach as the ideal way to integrate selection and assessment, career planning, management development, and succession planning, because these four systems have a common factor: Each deals with skills and abilities or competencies needed for successful job performance. Brush and Nardoni (1992) describe AT&T's integrated leadership system, which is designed to link succession planning, staffing, career development, and executive education.

11. The Succession Plan Emphasizes Accountability and Follow-up.

The potential impact of succession planning is often limited because of insufficient follow-up on planned actions, developmental plans in particular (Hall, 1986; Mahler & Drotter, 1986; Walker, 1980). According to Rothwell (1994), the "implementation of IDPs [individual developmental plans] is the Achilles' heel of many otherwise well-conceived succession planning programs" (p. 225). Thus, in addition to establishing planned activities, the succession plan should contain a time frame, which gives planned actions a deadline and a sense of urgency, and it should clearly delineate who is accountable for the implementation of specific developmental plans (Borwick, 1993; Hernandez et al., 1991; Rothwell, 1994).

Vetter (1984) suggests that each review session should result in specific outcomes that must be completed within the next twelve months by an accountable manager. Carnazza (1982) stresses that developmental plans should be formalized, and there should be a mechanism to ensure that these plans are implemented; in fact, Carnazza argues, this is one of the primary determinants of whether a succession plan will survive. To ensure accountability and follow-up on developmental plans, Rothwell (1994) suggests quarterly IDP meetings, wherein managers from each major area of the organization report on IDP progress in their areas. Or a succession-planning coordinator can periodically meet with individual managers to review progress on the IDPs in their area of responsibility.

Accountability can be increased by making specific outcomes of the succession plan visible, such as an annual report that summarizes the progress and outcomes of the succession plan (Mahler & Gaines, 1983). Some organizations present progress measures at their review meetings, such as the number of successors who actually filled jobs for which they were slated or the number of positions staffed through the use of the succession database (Buckner & Slavenski, 1994). Progress measures such as number of positions filled internally, time taken to fill these positions, and the effectiveness of individuals who fill these positions also demonstrate the "bottom-line value" of succession planning and help convey the importance of succession planning to top management (Rothwell, 1994).

Finally, and perhaps foremost, executives must recognize that development of their subordinates is one of their key responsibilities; although organizations tend to reward managers more for short-term performance than for long-term development efforts (Mahler, 1981; Vetter, 1984), managers should be evaluated and rewarded for their efforts to develop their employees (Friedman, 1986; Hall, 1989).

Accountability for development can be established by tying development to a bonus or appraisal system (Buckner & Slavenski, 1994; Hall, 1984, 1986; Hall & Foulkes, 1990; Hernandez et al., 1991; Hinrichs & Hollenbeck, 1990; Mahler & Drotter, 1986; Rhodes & Walker, 1984). At General Electric, for example, executives are held accountable for the development of managerial talent, and "people performance" is a factor when bonuses are determined (Friedman & LeVino, 1984).

Summary

The review of selected literature, represented by the eleven themes described above, has revealed several points: Although succession plans vary across organizations and should be tailored to an organization's unique needs, there are common elements that characterize effective succession-planning systems. Shared ownership of the succession plan throughout all layers of the organization is paramount: Top management provides visible support and conveys the message that succession planning is important; line management assumes active responsibility for the identification and development of talent; and staff provides functional support. Succession planning should be a flexible and evolving process which is intricately linked to the strategic business plan and designed to respond to changing organizational demands. Succession planning decisions should be based upon (a) well-defined requirements and competencies for upper-level positions (both current and projected) and (b) objective assessment data regarding employees' current performance and readiness or potential for future upper-level positions.

To operate most effectively, the succession plan should be closely linked with other personnel systems, such as performance appraisal, career development, and management development. The link between management development and succession planning is especially crucial, and providing succession candidates with challenging job assignments is a potent developmental strategy. Moreover, the planning process is more likely to satisfactorily meet the needs of both the organization and individual employees if information on employee career wishes and aspirations are factored into the succession plan. Finally, the succession plan should include provisions for follow-up on planned actions and should hold managers accountable for the development of their employees.

Author Index

Title Index

CENTER FOR CREATIVE LEADERSHIP PUBLICATIONS

SELECTED REPORTS:

Beyond Work-Family Programs J.R. Kofodimos (1995, Stock #167) $25.00

CEO Selection: A Street-Smart Review G.P. Hollenbeck (1994, Stock #164) $25.00

Coping With an Intolerable Boss M.M. Lombardo & M.W. McCall, Jr. (1984, Stock #305) $10.00

The Creative Opportunists: Conversations with the CEOs of Small Businesses
J.S. Bruce (1992, Stock #316) $12.00

Creativity in the R&D Laboratory T.M. Amabile & S.S. Gryskiewicz (1987, Stock #130) $12.00

Eighty-eight Assignments for Development in Place: Enhancing the Developmental
Challenge of Existing Jobs M.M. Lombardo & R.W. Eichinger (1989, Stock #136) $15.00

Enhancing 360-degree Feedback for Senior Executives: How to Maximize the Benefits and
Minimize the Risks R.E. Kaplan & C.J. Palus (1994, Stock #160) $15.00

An Evaluation of the Outcomes of a Leadership Development Program C.D. McCauley &
M.W. Hughes-James (1994, Stock #163) $35.00

Evolving Leaders: A Model for Promoting Leadership Development in Programs C.J. Palus &
W.H. Drath (1995, Stock #165) $20.00

Feedback to Managers, Volume I: A Guide to Evaluating Multi-rater Feedback Instruments
E. Van Velsor & J. Brittain Leslie (1991, Stock #149) $20.00

Feedback to Managers, Volume II: A Review and Comparison of Sixteen Multi-rater
Feedback Instruments E. Van Velsor & J. Brittain Leslie (1991, Stock #150) $80.00

Gender Differences in the Development of Managers: How Women Managers Learn From
Experience E. Van Velsor & M. W. Hughes (1990, Stock #145) $35.00

A Glass Ceiling Survey: Benchmarking Barriers and Practices A.M. Morrison, C.T. Schreiber,
& K.F. Price (1995, Stock #161) $20.00

High Hurdles: The Challenge of Executive Self-Development R.E. Kaplan, W.H. Drath, &
J.R. Kofodimos (1985, Stock #125) $15.00

The Intuitive Pragmatists: Conversations with Chief Executive Officers J.S. Bruce
(1986, Stock #310) $12.00

Key Events in Executives' Lives E.H. Lindsey, V. Homes, & M.W. McCall, Jr.
(1987, Stock #132) $65.00

Leadership for Turbulent Times L.R. Sayles (1995, Stock #325) $20.00

Learning How to Learn From Experience: Impact of Stress and Coping K.A. Bunker &
A.D. Webb (1992, Stock #154) $30.00

Making Common Sense: Leadership as Meaning-making in a Community of Practice
W.H. Drath & C.J. Palus (1994, Stock #156) $15.00

Off the Track: Why and How Successful Executives Get Derailed M.W. McCall, Jr., &
M.M. Lombardo (1983, Stock #121) $10.00

Preventing Derailment: What To Do Before It's Too Late M.M. Lombardo &
R.W. Eichinger (1989, Stock #138) $25.00

The Realities of Management Promotion M.N. Ruderman & P.J. Ohlott (1994, Stock #157) $20.00

Redefining What's Essential to Business Performance: Pathways to Productivity,
Quality, and Service L.R. Sayles (1990, Stock #142) $20.00

Succession Planning L.J. Eastman (1995, Stock #324) $20.00

Training for Action: A New Approach to Executive Development R.M. Burnside &
V.A. Guthrie (1992, Stock #153) $15.00

Traps and Pitfalls in the Judgment of Executive Potential M.N. Ruderman & P.J. Ohlott
(1990, Stock #141) $20.00

Twenty-two Ways to Develop Leadership in Staff Managers R.W. Eichinger & M.M. Lombardo
(1990, Stock #144) $15.00

Upward-communication Programs in American Industry A.I. Kraut & F.H. Freeman
(1992, Stock #152) $30.00

Using an Art Technique to Facilitate Leadership Development C. De Ciantis (1995, Stock #166)... $30.00

Why Executives Lose Their Balance J.R. Kofodimos (1989, Stock #137) $20.00

Why Managers Have Trouble Empowering: A Theoretical Perspective Based on Concepts of Adult Development W.H. Drath (1993, Stock #155) $15.00

SELECTED BOOKS:

Balancing Act: How Managers Can Integrate Successful Careers and Fulfilling Personal Lives J.R. Kofodimos (1993, Stock #247) $27.00

Beyond Ambition: How Driven Managers Can Lead Better and Live Better R.E. Kaplan, W.H. Drath, & J.R. Kofodimos (1991, Stock #227) $29.95

Breaking the Glass Ceiling: Can Women Reach the Top of America's Largest Corporations? (Updated Edition) A.M. Morrison, R.P. White, & E. Van Velsor (1992, Stock #236A) $12.50

Choosing to Lead K.E. Clark & M.B. Clark (1994, Stock #249) $35.00

Developing Diversity in Organizations: A Digest of Selected Literature A.M. Morrison & K.M. Crabtree (1992, Stock #317) $25.00

Discovering Creativity: Proceedings of the 1992 International Creativity and Innovation Networking Conference S.S. Gryskiewicz (Ed.) (1993, Stock #319) $30.00

Executive Selection: A Look at What We Know and What We Need to Know D.L. DeVries (1993, Stock #321) $20.00

Healing the Wounds: Overcoming the Trauma of Layoffs and Revitalizing Downsized Organizations D.M. Noer (1993, Stock #245) $26.00

If I'm In Charge Here, Why Is Everybody Laughing? D.P. Campbell (1980, Stock #205) $9.40

If You Don't Know Where You're Going You'll Probably End Up Somewhere Else D.P. Campbell (1974, Stock #203) $8.95

Inklings: Collected Columns on Leadership and Creativity D.P. Campbell (1992, Stock #233) $15.00

Leadership Education 1994-1995: A Source Book F.H. Freeman, K.B. Knott, & M.K. Schwartz (Eds.) (1994, Stock #322) $59.00

Leadership: Enhancing the Lessons of Experience R.L. Hughes, R.C. Ginnett, & G.J. Curphy (1992, Stock #246) $40.95

The Lessons of Experience: How Successful Executives Develop on the Job M.W. McCall, Jr., M.M. Lombardo, & A.M. Morrison (1988, Stock #211) $22.95

Making Diversity Happen: Controversies and Solutions A.M. Morrison, M.N. Ruderman, & M. Hughes-James (1993, Stock #320) $25.00

Measures of Leadership K.E. Clark & M.B. Clark (Eds.) (1990, Stock #215) $59.50

The New Leaders: Guidelines on Leadership Diversity in America A.M. Morrison (1992, Stock #238) $29.00

Readings in Innovation S.S. Gryskiewicz & D.A. Hills (Eds.) (1992, Stock #240) $25.00

Take the Road to Creativity and Get Off Your Dead End D.P. Campbell (1977, Stock #204) $8.95

Whatever It Takes: The Realities of Managerial Decision Making (Second Edition) M.W. McCall, Jr., & R.E. Kaplan (1990, Stock #218) $30.40

The Working Leader: The Triumph of High Performance Over Conventional Management Principles L.R. Sayles (1993, Stock #243) $24.95

SPECIAL PACKAGES:

Conversations with CEOs (includes 310 & 316) $16.00

Development & Derailment (includes 136, 138, & 144) $30.00

The Diversity Collection (includes 145, 236, 238, 317, & 320) $85.00

Executive Selection Package (includes 141, 321, & 157) $32.00

Feedback to Managers: Volumes I & II (includes 149 & 150) $85.00

Personal Growth, Taking Charge, and Enhancing Creativity (includes 203, 204, & 205) $20.00

Discounts are available. Please write for a comprehensive Publication & Products Catalog. Address your request to: Publication, Center for Creative Leadership, P.O. Box 26300, Greensboro, NC 27438-6300, 910-545-2805, or fax to 910-545-3221. All prices subject to change.

ORDER FORM

Name _____ Title _____

Organization _____

Mailing Address _____
(street address required for mailing)

City/State/Zip _____

Telephone _____ FAX _____
(telephone number required for UPS mailing)

Quantity	Stock No.	Title	Unit Cost	Amount

Subtotal	
Shipping and Handling (add 6% of subtotal with a $4.00 minimum; add 40% on all international shipping)	
NC residents add 6% sales tax; CA residents add 7% sales tax; CO residents add 6.2% sales tax	
TOTAL	

METHOD OF PAYMENT

❏ Check or money order enclosed (payable to Center for Creative Leadership).

❏ Purchase Order No. _____ (Must be accompanied by this form.)

❏ Charge my order, plus shipping, to my credit card:
      ❏ American Express ❏ Discover ❏ MasterCard ❏ VISA

ACCOUNT NUMBER:_____ EXPIRATION DATE: MO.___ YR.___

NAME OF ISSUING BANK: _____

SIGNATURE _____

❏ Please put me on your mailing list.
❏ Please send me the Center's quarterly newsletter, *Issues & Observations*.

Publication • Center for Creative Leadership • P.O. Box 26300
Greensboro, NC 27438-6300
910-545-2805 • FAX 910-545-3221

Client Priority Code: R

fold here

PLACE
STAMP
HERE

CENTER FOR CREATIVE LEADERSHIP
PUBLICATION
P.O. Box 26300
Greensboro, NC 27438-6300